MW00561294

מאמר
מי כמוכה
תרכ"ט

TRUE EXISTENCE

מאמר

מי כמוכה

תרכ"ט

TRUE EXISTENCE

a chasidic discourse by

Rabbi Shmuel Schneersohn

זצוקללה"ה נבג"מ זי"ע

of Lubavitch

•

translated and annotated by

Rabbi Yosef Marcus

annotated by

Rabbi Avraham D. Vaisfiche

Kehot Publication Society

770 Eastern Parkway / Brooklyn, New York, 11213

True Existence

Published and Copyrighted © 2002
Third Printing—January 2021
by
Kehot Publication Society
770 Eastern Parkway / Brooklyn, New York 11213
(718) 774-4000 / Fax (718) 774-2718
editor@kehot.com / www.kehot.org

Orders:
291 Kingston Avenue / Brooklyn, New York 11213
(718) 778-0226 / Fax (718) 778-4148
www.kehot.com

3 5 7 9 11 12 10 8 6 4

LC Record available at: https://lccn.loc.gov/2007281411

ISBN 978-0-8266-0461-3

Manufactured in the United States of America

CONTENTS

ב"ה

PREFACE

We are delighted to present the fifth volume in the Chasidic Heritage Series, an English rendition of the famous discourse entitled: *Mi Chamocha 5629.* The present bi-lingual edition has been subtitled *True Existence.*

Said in 5629 [1869] by the fourth Lubavitcher Rebbe, Rabbi Shmuel of Lubavitch, this discourse revolutionizes the age-old notion of Monotheism, i.e., that there is no other god besides Him. Supported by Talmudic and Midrashic statements, the discourse demonstrates how not only is there no other god besides Him, there is nothing besides Him —literally. The only thing that truly exists is G-d.

The masters of Chabad Chasidism wrote, and frequently repeated, discourses designated for the purpose of mystically cleansing the atmosphere. It was the present discourse that Rabbi Shmuel would often review for the purpose of purifying the spiritual environment.

In addition to the translation of the discourse by Rabbi Yosef Marcus, extensive annotations were added by Rabbi Avraham D. Vaisfiche to clarify the obscure concepts referred to in the text. The Hebrew text of the discourse has been retypeset with Hebrew vowel marks to further enhance this volume's usability. A brief biography of the author's life has been added as an appendix.

Special thanks are due to Rabbis Yosef B. Friedman, Shmuel Marcus, Manis Friedman, and Dovid Olidort for their editorial assistance.

Kehot Publication Society

3 Tammuz 5762

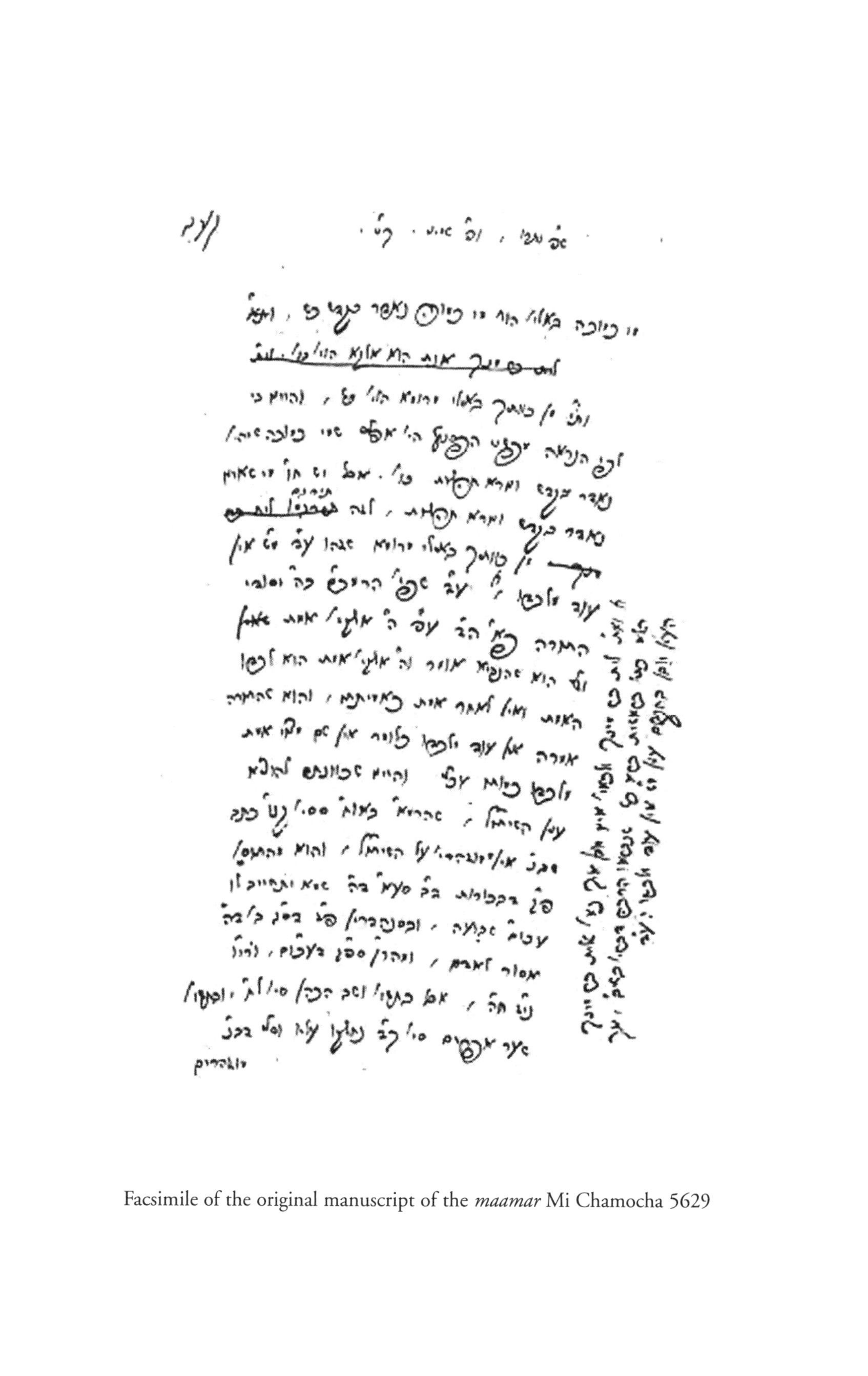

Facsimile of the original manuscript of the *maamar* Mi Chamocha 5629

INTRODUCTION AND SUMMARY

INTRODUCTION AND SUMMARY

There is None Besides Him

> *A Chasidic lumber merchant in Riga was calculating his accounts. Under a column of figures he inadvertently wrote, "Total:* Ein od milvado!*—There is none besides Him!" In response to his assistant's raised eyebrow he said: "During prayer it is considered perfectly natural to let one's mind wander off to his lumber in Riga. So what is so surprising if in the middle of business dealings the mind is invaded by thoughts of the unity of G-d?"*
>
> *—Chasidic Story*

It is perhaps the most oft-quoted phrase in Chabad Chasidism: *ein od milvado*—there is none besides Him. It is a three-word phrase that encapsulates an entire philosophy. It is a notion that every chasid strives to absorb.

In its common interpretation, the phrase expresses the fundamental Jewish belief that there is no other god besides Him. Monotheism. It expresses the same idea as "Hear O Israel the L-rd is our G-d, the L-rd is one."

But in Chabad philosophy, the phrase means much more. Not only is there no other *god* besides Him, there is *nothing* besides Him—literally. Only G-d exists. This is a statement on the nature of the cosmos as much as it is a theological belief.

What of the world and all that is in it? What of the empirical sightings of our fleshly eye? Is it only an illusion?

No. The Torah states clearly: *In the beginning G-d created the heaven and the earth.* For six days He created things. These things exist really, for if the world is not real, then Torah, indeed life itself, is meaningless. Such a notion is untenable.

How then to reconcile our perception of reality with *ein od milvado*? The Alter Rebbe, Rabbi Schneur Zalman of Liadi, founder of Chabad Chasidism, explains it this way (*Shaar Hayichud v'haEmunah* III):

> If the eye were allowed to perceive the life and spirit that is in every created being—which courses within it from the utterance of G-d's mouth—then the corporeality and tangibility of the created being would not be perceived by our eyes at all. For it is literally null in relation to the life and spirit that it contains, since without the spirit it is literally naught, a nonentity, as it was before the Six Days of Creation. The spirit that flows to it from the mouth of G-d is the only thing that removes it constantly from nothingness and brings it into being.

It follows, then, that there is nothing besides Him—truly. The Alter Rebbe establishes that the world and all its contents exist only by virtue of the fact that G-d is constantly creating them. Were He for one moment to cease creating, all of creation would lose its existence. It would not crumble, or burn up, or dissolve—it would simply cease to exist, as if it had never existed.

PERPETUAL CREATION

Forever, O G-d, Your word stands firm in the heavens, says the psalmist.[1] The Baal Shem Tov would cite the Midrash[2]: *Your words that you spoke, Let there be a firmament—these words continue to stand in the heavens to create them.* And just as words exist only as long as they are being uttered, so the world, created by G-d's mouth, must be constantly uttered into existence.

For the existence of the world—created from nothing—was and is a miracle. It was and is "unnatural." And just as we don't expect miracles to go on indefinitely—we expect the waters of the sea to return to their natural flow after G-d is finished holding them up for the Israelites—so should we not

---

1. Psalms 119:89.

2. *Midrash Tehillim* on the verse.

expect the world to continue to exist. We should expect it to return to its natural state: nonexistence.

When you throw a rock in the air, you don't expect it to stay there. As soon as the power of your throw invested in the rock dissipates, the rock returns to its natural state: inert.

So, yes, the world exists. But its existence is entirely dependent upon the Divine word that commands its existence. Such "existence" cannot compete with *true* existence, one that is not dependent on any other being: the absolute existence of G-d. The existence of the world is not self-attributable. Even as it exists, it is not truly existent—just as the airborne rock has not become "a flying rock." The world does not take on the properties of existence even as it exists.

Maimonides says as much in the second chapter of his *Laws of the Foundations of Torah*:

> This is what the prophet means with "G-d is true." He alone is true, and no other being possesses truth like His truth. This is what the Torah says: *ein od milvado*—i.e., there is no other *true* existence besides Him that is like Him.

This doctrine of "perpetual creation" provided a rational foundation to the Baal Shem Tov's motto: G-d is everywhere. His opponents argued, How can you put G-d in the trash bin? The Alter Rebbe said, How can a trash bin exist without a Divine directive invested in it?[3]

Before and during prayer the Chabad chasid will meditate on *ein od milvado*. He will contemplate the words of the *Zohar*: *No place is devoid of Him*. G-d is immanent. He will break into song about it in the late hours of a *farbrengen*. He will spend his entire lifetime internalizing this notion—a notion that runs contrary to his sensorly perception.

This is his task.

---

3. It should be noted that even according to Chasidic philosophy, G-d—being beyond all rational rules—could theoretically have created a world separate from Him which would at the same time not contradict *ein od milvado*, yet He chose to be perpetually involved. (see *Sefer Hamaamarim 5643*, p. 35 ff; *Torat Menachem – Hadranim al Harambam v'Shas*, p. 43 ff.).

ROOSTER'S CROW

Each of the Chabad masters had a particular discourse that he would repeat every two or three years. This they did in order to "purify the environment." The recurring discourse of the fourth Rebbe, Rabbi Shmuel, concerned *ein od milvado.*[4]

The present discourse entitled *Who is like You* of 5629 (1869), begins with a lengthy discussion on the spiritual roots of physical phenomena. The human eye beholds what is essentially the final and lowest manifestation of supernal, spiritual phenomena. Everything in this world has its source and counterpart in the spiritual realms. The early morning crow of the rooster is a reverberation of spiritual stirrings in the supernal world of *Atzilut* and beyond. Day and night are the reflections of the two types of celestial song. (Thus Moses knew day from night during his forays into heaven.)

The Rebbe uses this concept to make sense of a number of otherwise cryptic Midrashic statements. The Midrash says[5] that G-d created the world with snow and earth from beneath the Throne of Glory. According to the Rebbe, these statements refer to the spiritual origins of physical phenomena. In like vein, Talmudic tales[6] about talking grass are understood as references to the spiritual antecedents of grass, the angels (who can certainly speak).

Myriad levels of evolvement stand between the original, spiritual form of an entity and its physical form. Yet no amount of evolvement can produce a corporeal being out of a spiritual being. Between the lowest spiritual level and the highest physical level there is still an unbridgeable gap that must be closed. This is where "something from nothing" must be introduced. Up until this point, each level is within the realm of the one above it—like a chain, whose every link is ultimately attached to all the links. At this point there is a break—the physical reality is not linked to its spiritual source, the source is concealed from it. There is no point of contact

---

4. *Hayom Yom* 28 Tammuz.

5. *Pirkei d'Rabbi Eliezer,* chap. 3.

6. *Chullin* 60a.

7. *Sanhedrin* 38b.

between them. It is this concealment that creates the physical reality. Without this concealment, the coarse physical reality would not be visible: "*the corporeality and tangibility of the created being would not be perceived by our eyes at all.*"

Hence is explained another mysterious statement in the Talmud[7] about G-d "extending His small finger among the angels and consuming them." According to the Rebbe, this refers to G-d revealing more of their origins than they can handle. This revelation causes them to lose their existence.

In fact all of existence will reach this state of nonexistence in the "millennia of destruction" mentioned in the Talmud.[8] At that point, Divine revelation will be such that physical reality will cease to exist. Thus, the Rebbe concludes, even now the world is not truly existent. For true existence is everlasting.

(The Rebbe cites a halachic corollary to this concept: A body of water that dries up once in seven years does not have the halachic status of "living (running) water"—even while it is running. A temporary existence is not true existence.)

FOUR ELEMENTS

The Rebbe then takes it a step further. Physical entities are not physical. Each physical entity is made up of four[9] elements: fire, water, air and earth. But its being is none of the four. Its being is the power of amalgamation that fuses the four elements into a physical being. And what is that power? The Divine "word." Isolate each of the elements and you are left with nothing.

ONE AND ONLY

The Chabad conception of *ein od milvado*, the Rebbe continues, also accounts for the use of the word *echad*, "one," in the verse *Hear O Israel the L-rd is our G-d, the L-rd is one.*[10] It would seem that the word *yachid* (single, alone) would better

---

8. *Sanhedrin* 97a.

9. See *Likkutei Sichot*, vol. 38 p. 184.

10. Deuteronomy 6:4.

convey the Oneness of G-d, since the word *echad* also has the connotation of "one of many."

But that is precisely why *echad* is used. The Talmud states[11] that the three letters of the word *echad* symbolize the seven heavens and one earth (alluded to in the *chet*—numerically equivalent to 8—of *echad*), the four corners of the world (alluded to in the *dalet* (4) of *echad*), and the One G-d, Master of all (alluded to in the *alef*, which connotes rulership). So the use of the word *echad* intimates that even in the realm of many—the seven heavens and one earth, and the four corners of the world, G-d is still the only one. He is not just one outside of reality, *yachid*; He is one even within the context of supposed otherness.

The 8 and the 4 are entirely nullified to the Alef—the One G-d. *Ein od milvado.*

NOTE ON THE HEBREW TEXT: In vowelizing the Hebrew words in this edition we have followed the grammatical rules of the Holy Tongue, which occasionally differ from the traditional or colloquial pronunciation. The original footnotes to the Hebrew text appear at the end of the maamar.

11. *Berachot* 13b.

TRANSLATION
AND
COMMENTARY

With the help of Heaven. Shabbat parshat Yitro and parshat Shemini, [56]29.

"WHO IS LIKE YOU AMONG THE *EILIM*, O G-D! WHO IS LIKE YOU, RESPLENDENT IN HOLINESS..."[1]

Yonathan[2] translates this as, "Who is like You among the supernal beings, O G-d..." Without his translation the verse can be understood to mean that there is none like You resplendent in holiness and awesome in praise—but there is, Heaven forbid, another god, albeit one that is not resplendent in holiness and awesome in praise. Yonathan therefore translates it as, "Who is like You *among the supernal beings*," so that the verse conveys the same idea as the verse,[3] "There is nothing else besides Him."[4] Onkelos[5] translates it as "There is nothing besides You."

Now, how can it be said that "there is nothing else besides You" when it is written, "In the beginning G-d created...,"[6] which implies that many things were created during the six days of creation?[7]

---

1. Exodus 15:11.

2. Yonathan ben Uziel, a disciple of Hillel the Elder, authored an Aramaic translation/commentary on the Torah (circa 50 c.e.). The Talmud (*Megillah* 3b) relates that upon concluding his translation of the Prophets, a storm of criticism arose that rocked the land of Israel. A Heavenly voice rang out: "Who revealed My secrets to mankind?" Whereupon Yonathan ben Uziel arose and proclaimed, "It was I who revealed Your secrets. It is revealed and known before You that I did not do it for my own honor nor for that of my father's house, but for Your honor, in order that disputes should not multiply in Israel!" He wished to continue and translate the Writings too, but a Heavenly voice called out, "Enough!"

3. Deuteronomy 4:35. This phrase is often understood to mean that there is no *god* outside of G-d. The Rebbe, however, like Rambam (cited below), understands it to mean that *nothing* exists besides G-d.

4. "Who is like You among the supernal beings" is understood to mean that the reality of G-d's existence is unlike that of any other being, since everything else is dependent on G-d for its existence. This is the same idea as "there is nothing else besides Him," i.e., nothing that enjoys an independent existence. The following is the opening phrases of a similar *maamar*

בס״ד. שַׁבָּת פָּרָשַׁת יִתְרוֹ וּפָרָשַׁת שְׁמִינִי, [תר]ך״ט.

מִי כָמוֹכָה בָּאֵלִים הוי׳ מִי כָּמוֹכָה נֶאְדָּר בַּקֹּדֶשׁ כו׳,

וְתִרְגֵּם יוֹנָתָן מָן כְּוָותָךְ בְּאֵילֵי מְרוֹמָא הוי׳ כו׳, וְהַיְינוּ כִּי לְפִי הַנִּרְאֶה מִפְּשַׁט הַפָּסוּק הָיָה אֶפְשָׁר לוֹמַר שֶׁמִּי כָּמוֹכָה שֶׁיִּהְיֶה נֶאְדָּר בַּקֹּדֶשׁ וְנוֹרָא תְהִלּוֹת כו׳, אֲבָל יֵשׁ חַס וְשָׁלוֹם מִי שֶׁאֵינוֹ נֶאְדָּר בַּקֹּדֶשׁ וְנוֹרָא תְהִלּוֹת, לָזֶה תִּירְגֵּם מָן כְּוָותָךְ בְּאֵילֵי מְרוֹמָא שֶׁזֶּהוּ עַל דֶּרֶךְ מַה שֶּׁכָּתוּב אֵין עוֹד מִלְּבַדּוֹ. וְאוּנְקְלוּס תִּירְגֵּם לֵית בַּר מִינָּךְ,

וְלִכְאוֹרָה אֵינוֹ מוּבָן אֵיךְ נֶאֱמַר שֶׁלֵּית בַּר מִינָּךְ הֲלֹא כְּתִיב בְּרֵאשִׁית בָּרָא כו׳ שֶׁנִּבְרְאוּ הַרְבֵּה דְּבָרִים בְּשֵׁשֶׁת יְמֵי בְרֵאשִׁית.

---

by Rabbi Shmuel (*Or Hatorah, B'shalach* p. 547; *Sefer Hamaamarim 5627* (Ed. 2000) p. 487):

"Who is like You among the *eilim*..." *Yonathan* translates this as, "Who is like You among the supernal beings..." (Rashi translates "among the *eilim*" as "among the mighty ones.") At first glance, the verse seems incomprehensible. For it seems to read, "Who is *like You* among the gods, O G-d, i.e., there is none like You among the gods, but there exists a god, G-d forbid, albeit not like You. Or, a god that is "*resplendent in holiness*" cannot be found, but one that is *not* resplendent in holiness, can be found. Thus, *Yonathan* translates *eilim* as "supernal beings," i.e., there is none like You *among the angels*.... See also *U'Sfartem Lachem* in *Sefer Hamaamarim 5736* p. 213 ff.

5. Onkelos (2nd century c.e.), a proselyte of Roman origin, authored *Targum Onkelos*, an Aramaic translation of the Torah, under the guidance of Rabbi Eliezer (see fn. 42) and Rabbi Yehoshua. Rashi (*Kiddushin* 49a, s.v. *harei zeh mecharef*) says of him that he "did not add anything to the Torah, and is therefore not considered a blasphemer, because it was all given at Mount Sinai. It was subsequently forgotten and he restated it, as recounted in Tractate *Megillah* (3a)."

6. Genesis 1:1.

7. Rabbi Shmuel does not cite "empirical" evidence, which can be debated. He considers a verse in the Torah to be far more compelling.

We can understand this by explaining the verse, "There is nothing else besides Him" as Rambam interprets it in his *Laws of the Foundations of Torah* (1:4), in explanation of the verse, "The L-rd, G-d, is true"[8]:

> This is what the prophet means with the words "The L-rd, G-d is true," meaning that He alone is true and no other being possesses truth like His truth. This is what the Torah means with the words, "There is nothing else besides Him," meaning that there is no true being besides Him that is like Him.

In the above passage, Rambam wishes to negate the concept of *sheetuf.*[9] By contrast, the Children of Noah,[10] Rama[11] rules, are not obligated to reject *sheetuf* (*Orach Chaim,*[12] 156, end). He derives this from *Tosafot* (first chapter of *Bechorot,* 2a end, s.v. *shema yitchayev lo akum shevuah,* and *Sanhedrin* chapter seven, 63b, s.v. *asur l'adam*), and from Ran[13] (end of first chapter of tractate *Avodat Kochavim*[14]), and *Riv,*[15] *n'tiv* 17, *chelek* 5. However, in the responsa *Veshav Hakohen*[16] (38), and the responsa *Shaar Ephraim*[17] (204), these authors

8. Jeremiah 10:10.

9. SHEETUF. The belief that a given being has power, albeit one that is inferior to the Supreme Being. This is not idolatry, i.e., considering a being to be *equal* to G-d. Rather, *sheetuf* means to consider an entity to be a *partner* to G-d, i.e., to ascribe power to another being besides G-d, even while accepting G-d as the Supreme Being.

Below, Rabbi Shmuel will elaborate on the concept of *sheetuf* and the verse in the Torah that negates it. By doing so he will provide reason for Onkelos' translation, "There is nothing besides You."

10. I.e., non-Jews. The Children of Noah are obligated to keep the following seven laws, known as the Seven Laws of Noah: the prohibitions against idolatry, adultery, murder, blasphemy, theft, causing pain to animals—and the obligation to set up a court system. Rabbi Shmuel will now cite the various opinions as to whether the belief in *sheetuf* is considered idolatry for a non-Jew.

11. Rabbi Moses Isserles of Cracow, Poland (1530 – 1572). Author of many works and recognized as the pre-eminent halachic authority throughout the Ashkenazic community. Most famous are his Ashkenazic annotations to Rabbi Yosef Caro's *Shulchan Aruch,* which transformed this predominantly Sephardic work into a universal Code of Jewish Law. He was well versed in Jewish philosophy and Kabbalah, and authored a commentary on the Zohar.

12. Lit. "Way of Life." The section of the Code of Jewish Law dealing with daily conduct and the yearly cycle, such as the laws of Prayer, Blessings, Shabbat and Festivals.

13. Rabbenu Nissim of Barcelona, Spain

אַךְ הָעִנְיָן יוּבַן בְּהֶקְדֵּם עִנְיַן מַה שֶּׁכָּתוּב אֵין עוֹד מִלְּבַדּוֹ עַל דֶּרֶךְ שֶׁפֵּירֵשׁ הָרַמְבַּ"ם בְּהִלְכוֹת יְסוֹדֵי הַתּוֹרָה פֶּרֶק א הֲלָכָה ד עַל פָּסוּק וַה' אֱלֹקִים אֱמֶת,

וְזֶה לְשׁוֹנוֹ הוּא שֶׁהַנָּבִיא אוֹמֵר וַה' אֱלֹקִים אֱמֶת הוּא לְבַדּוֹ הָאֱמֶת וְאֵין לְאַחֵר אֱמֶת כַּאֲמִיתָּתוֹ, וְהוּא שֶׁהַתּוֹרָה אָמְרָה אֵין עוֹד מִלְּבַדּוֹ כְּלוֹמַר אֵין שָׁם מָצוּי אֱמֶת מִלְּבַדּוֹ כְּמוֹתוֹ עַד כַּאן לְשׁוֹנוֹ,

וְהַיְינוּ שֶׁכַּוָּונָתוֹ לְהוֹצִיא עִנְיַן הַשִּׁיתּוּף, שֶׁהָרְמָ"א בְּאוֹרַח חַיִּים סוֹף סִימָן קנ"ו כָּתַב שֶׁבְּנֵי נֹחַ אֵין מוּזְהָרִים עַל הַשִּׁיתּוּף, וְהוּא מֵהַתּוֹסְפוֹת פֶּרֶק קַמָּא דִּבְכוֹרוֹת דַּף ב סוֹף עַמּוּד א דִּבּוּר הַמַּתְחִיל שֶׁמָּא יִתְחַיֵּיב לוֹ עַכּוּ"ם [עוֹבֵד כּוֹכָבִים וּמַזָּלוֹת] שְׁבוּעָה, וּבְסַנְהֶדְרִין פֶּרֶק ז דַּף ס"ג עַמּוּד ב דִּבּוּר הַמַּתְחִיל אָסוּר לְאָדָם, וּמֵהָרַ"ן סוֹף פֶּרֶק קַמָּא דְּעַכּוּ"ם,

---

(1290 – 1375). Famous for his extensive commentary to *The Book of Laws* by Rabbi Yitzchak Alfasi, known as the Rif, printed in the back of many Talmudic tractates. He also authored a collection of homiletic discourses discussing the essentials of Jewish faith, a partial commentary to the Torah and liturgical hymns.

14. More commonly known as *Avodah Zarah*, which translates as "foreign worship." *Avodat Kochavim*, "worship of the stars," was a euphemism used to bypass the censors.

15. *Riv* is an acronym given by the halachists and codifiers for Rabbenu Yerucham (c. 1280 – c. 1350), a disciple of the Rosh, who lived in Provence and Spain. He compiled halachic works dealing with financial matters and the Jewish lifecycle. The latter, named *Toldot Adam V'Chava*, is a work consisting of two parts. The first part, *Adam*, discusses all the laws that pertain from birth until marriage; the second, *Chava*, with all the laws that pertain from marriage until death. They are divided into *n'tivim* (paths), which are subdivided into *chalakim* (portions).

16. The author, Rabbi Refoel *Hakohen* (1723 – 1804), was the Rabbi of the tri-communities of Altona, Hamburg, and Wandsbeck in Germany, known by their Hebrew acronym "AHU," or "AHUV" ("beloved"). He entitled his responsa "and the *kohen* shall return (or 'respond')," a play on the words (Lev. 14:39) describing the kohen's return visit to the *metzora*.

17. The author, Rabbi Ephraim Katz (1616 – 1678), served in the Rabbinic Court of Vilna until the Cossack invasion of 1655. Wandering across Europe, he was finally appointed as Rabbi of Ofen (Budapest) in 1666. He wrote halachic responsa to such distant places as Turkey and Jerusalem.

differ with Rama, maintaining that the Children of Noah are included in the prohibition on belief in *sheetuf.*

NOT IDOLATRY

[The argument regarding the Children of Noah stems from the fact that] *sheetuf* is not idolatry. As our Sages comment (*Midrash Rabbah* 1[:3]) regarding the angels:

> Rabbi Yochanan says they were created on the second day of creation. Rabbi Chanina says they were created on the fifth. [As the Torah states regarding the fifth day, G-d created] "fowl that fly."[18] *Fowl* refers to the angel Michael; *that fly* refers to Gabriel. Rabbi Lulina son of Tavrin said: Both Rabbi Chanina and Rabbi Yochanan agree that no angels were created on the first day so that people would not say "Michael...on the south and Gabriel on the north and G-d ... in the middle." This idea is expressed in the verse, "I am G-d, Creator of all.... Who was with Me?"[19]—i.e., who was a partner with Me in Creation?

We can infer from this Midrash that ascribing power to angels, e.g., Michael and Gabriel, would also be considered *sheetuf,* even though [one recognizes that] they are *created* beings. Thus, had they been created on the first day, it could have been said that they were partners, Heaven forbid, in Creation. They were therefore created on the second or fifth day so that it should not be said that they were partners, Heaven forbid.

PARTNERS

If so, *sheetuf* is not like idolatry. For even if the angels would have been created on the first day, one would not, Heaven forbid, ascribe deity to them, since [one recognizes that] they are created beings. Rather, one would use the term *partner.* So we see that *sheetuf* is not like idolatry. Rather, like our Sages state, "Three partners [contribute to the creation] of man: the father and mother... [provide the body] ...and G-d provides the soul."[20]

So we see that although G-d provides the primary aspect of the human—for as soon as the soul leaves the body, the contribution of

---

18. Genesis 1:20.

19. Isaiah 44:24.

וְרַבֵּנוּ יְרוּחָם נָתִיב י״ז חֵלֶק ה. אֲבָל בִּתְשׁוּבַת וְשָׁב הַכֹּהֵן סִימָן ל״ח, וּבִתְשׁוּבַת שַׁעַר אֶפְרַיִם סִימָן ד״ד נֶחְלְקוּ עָלָיו וּסְבִירָא לְהוּ דִּבְנֵי נֹחַ מוּזְהָרִים עַל הַשִּׁיתּוּף.

וְהַיְינוּ כִּי עִנְיַן הַשִּׁיתּוּף אֵינוֹ עֲבוֹדָה זָרָה כְּלָל, אֶלָּא עַל דֶּרֶךְ שֶׁאָמְרוּ רַבּוֹתֵינוּ זִכְרוֹנָם לִבְרָכָה בְּמִדְרָשׁ רַבָּה פַּרְשָׁה א בְּעִנְיַן הַמַּלְאָכִים

שֶׁרַבִּי יוֹחָנָן אוֹמֵר שֶׁנִּבְרְאוּ בַּשֵּׁנִי וְרַבִּי חֲנִינָא אוֹמֵר שֶׁנִּבְרְאוּ בַּחֲמִישִׁי וְעוֹף יְעוֹפֵף, וְעוֹף זֶה מִיכָאֵל יְעוֹפֵף זֶה גַּבְרִיאֵל, אָמַר רַבִּי לוּלִיָנָא בַּר טַבְרִין בֵּין עַל דַּעְתּוֹ דְרַבִּי חֲנִינָא בֵּין עַל דַּעְתּוֹ דְרַבִּי יוֹחָנָן הַכֹּל מוֹדִים שֶׁלֹּא נִבְרָא בָּרִאשׁוֹן כְּלוּם שֶׁלֹּא יֹאמְרוּ שֶׁמִּיכָאֵל מוֹתֵחַ בִּדְרוֹמוֹ וְגַבְרִיאֵל בִּצְפוֹנוֹ וְהַקָּדוֹשׁ בָּרוּךְ הוּא מְמַדֵּד בְּאֶמְצַע, הֲדָא הוּא דִכְתִיב אָנֹכִי ה׳ עוֹשֶׂה כֹּל מִי אִתִּי, מִי הָיָה שׁוּתָּף אִתִּי בְּמַעֲשֵׂה בְרֵאשִׁית.

נִשְׁמָע מִזֶּה שֶׁעִנְיַן הַשִּׁיתּוּף יִתָּכֵן גַּם עַל הַמַּלְאָכִים מִיכָאֵל וְגַבְרִיאֵל שֶׁהֵם נִבְרָאִים וְאִם הָיוּ נִבְרָאִים בָּרִאשׁוֹן הָיוּ יְכוֹלִים לוֹמַר שֶׁהָיוּ שׁוּתָּפִים חַס וְשָׁלוֹם בְּמַעֲשֵׂה בְרֵאשִׁית לָזֶה נִבְרְאוּ בַּשֵּׁנִי אוֹ בַחֲמִישִׁי שֶׁלֹּא יֹאמְרוּ שֶׁהֵם שׁוּתָּפִים חַס וְשָׁלוֹם,

וְאִם כֵּן עִנְיַן הַשִּׁיתּוּף אֵינוֹ כְּמוֹ עֲבוֹדָה זָרָה, שֶׁמֵּאַחַר שֶׁהֵם נִבְרָאִים הִנֵּה אֲפִילוּ אִם הָיוּ נִבְרָאִים בָּרִאשׁוֹן גַּם כֵּן אֵינוֹ נוֹפֵל לֵאמֹר עֲלֵיהֶם חַס וְשָׁלוֹם לְשׁוֹן אֱלֹקִים כִּי אִם לְשׁוֹן שִׁיתּוּף, וְנִמְצָא מוּבָן שֶׁעִנְיַן הַשִּׁיתּוּף אֵינוֹ כְּמוֹ עֲבוֹדָה זָרָה, אֶלָּא עַל דֶּרֶךְ שֶׁאָמְרוּ רַבּוֹתֵינוּ זִכְרוֹנָם לִבְרָכָה ג׳ שׁוּתָּפִין בָּאָדָם אָב וָאֵם כו׳ וְהַקָּדוֹשׁ בָּרוּךְ הוּא נוֹתֵן בּוֹ נְשָׁמָה

הִנֵּה הֲגַם שֶׁחֵלֶק הַקָּדוֹשׁ בָּרוּךְ הוּא הוּא הָעִיקָּר שֶׁהֲרֵי בְּצֵאת הַנֶּפֶשׁ מִן הַגּוּף הֲרֵי מוּטָל חֵלֶק אָב וָאֵם כְּאֶבֶן דּוֹמֵם,

20. *Niddah* 31a.

the parents lies motionless as a stone—and their contribution does not compare to G-d's, which creates the person and his life, nevertheless, G-d granted them honor, as in the verse, "Honor your father and mother,"[21] as we will explain, please G-d. So the parents are called "partners"; and in a similar way *sheetuf* means that one "combines the Name of G-d" [with something else], but it is not idolatry.

Now we can understand the saying of our Sages (*Midrash Rabbah*[22]): "Adam received six commandments[23] and one of them was the prohibition against idolatry." Now if *sheetuf* is synonymous with idolatry, how can Tosafot, Ran, Riv and Rama say that the Children of Noah are not obligated to reject *sheetuf*, when in fact idolatry was made forbidden to Adam? Rather, as we said earlier, *sheetuf* is not idolatry at all. Rather, it is like [comparing G-d to] a king that is the supreme ruler over his countrymen, who, nevertheless, grants honor to the ministers who live throughout the states of his kingdom.

Furthermore, the prohibition against idolatry is derived from the verse, "You shall not have other gods before Me,"[24] while the prohibition against belief in *sheetuf* stems from the commandment obligating one to believe that G-d is one. This commandment is derived from the verse, "Hear, O Israel...G-d is one,"[25] as Rambam, Semag,[26] and Ra'ah[27] write in their enumeration of the commandments.[28] This is because the prohibition against belief in *sheetuf* is deduced from the commandment to believe that G-d is one, which in turn is derived from the verse, "G-d is one."

---

21. Exodus 20:12.

22. *Devarim Rabbah* 2:17.

23. The seven commandments of Noah excluding the prohibition against paining animals. The latter commandment was given to Noah after the Flood, when the consumption of animals was permitted.

24. Exodus 20:3.

25. Deuteronomy 6:4.

26. An acronym for *Sefer Mitzvot Gadol*, a work that provides a description and explanation of the 613 commandments, by Rabbi Moses of Coucy (13th century). *Semag's* publication in 1489 preceded the Shulchan Aruch, and its author was thus considered a leading halachic authority at that time. Rabbi Moses, a brilliant orator, traveled across France and Spain inspiring the populace to the service of G-d.

וְאֵינוֹ בְּעֵרֶךְ לְחֵלֶק הַקָּדוֹשׁ בָּרוּךְ הוּא שֶׁהוּא הָאָדָם וְחַיּוּתוֹ, וּמִכָּל מָקוֹם חָלַק לָהֶם כָּבוֹד כְּמוֹ שֶׁכָּתוּב כַּבֵּד אֶת אָבִיךָ וְאֶת אִמֶּךָ, וּכְמוֹ שֶׁיִּתְבָּאֵר אִם יִרְצֶה ה׳, וְנִקְרָאִים שׁוּתָּפִים, וְעַל דֶּרֶךְ זֶה הוּא עִנְיַן הַשִּׁיתּוּף שֶׁמְּשַׁתְּפִים לְשֵׁם שָׁמַיִם כו׳ אֲבָל אֵינוֹ עֲבוֹדָה זָרָה.

וּבָזֶה יוּבַן מַאֲמַר רַבּוֹתֵינוּ זִכְרוֹנָם לִבְרָכָה בְּמִדְרָשׁ רַבָּה שִׁשָּׁה דְבָרִים נִצְטַוָּה אָדָם הָרִאשׁוֹן וְאֶחָד מֵהֶם הוּא עֲבוֹדָה זָרָה, וְאִם נֹאמַר שֶׁשִּׁיתּוּף הוּא עֲבוֹדָה זָרָה הֵאיךְ יִסְבְּרוּ הַתּוֹסְפוֹת וְהָרַ״ן וְרַבֵּנוּ יְרוּחָם וְהָרְמָ״א שֶׁבְּנֵי נֹחַ אֵינָם מוּזְהָרִים עַל הַשִּׁיתּוּף מֵאַחַר שֶׁאָדָם הָרִאשׁוֹן נִצְטַוָּה עַל זֶה. אַךְ הָעִנְיָן הוּא כַּנַּ״ל [כְּנִזְכָּר לְעֵיל] שֶׁהַשִּׁיתּוּף אֵינוֹ עֲבוֹדָה זָרָה כְּלָל, כִּי אִם כְּמוֹ שֶׁהַמֶּלֶךְ הוּא אֶחָד עַל כָּל בְּנֵי מְדִינָתוֹ וּמִכָּל מָקוֹם חוֹלֵק כָּבוֹד לְהַשָּׂרִים אֲשֶׁר בְּכָל מְדִינוֹת מַלְכוּתוֹ כו׳,

וּבֶאֱמֶת לָאו דַּעֲבוֹדָה זָרָה הוּא מִפָּסוּק לֹא יִהְיֶה לְךָ אֱלֹקִים אֲחֵרִים עַל פָּנָי, וְעִנְיַן הַשִּׁיתּוּף הוּא מִמִּצְוַת לְיַיחֲדוֹ שֶׁיּוֹצֵא מִפָּסוּק שְׁמַע יִשְׂרָאֵל כו׳ ה׳ אֶחָד, כְּמוֹ שֶׁכָּתְבוּ הָרַמְבַּ״ם וְהַסְּמַ״ג וְהָרְאָ״ה זִכְרוֹנָם לִבְרָכָה בְּמִנְיַן הַמִּצְוֹת, וְהַיְינוּ כִּי מִצְוַת לְיַיחֲדוֹ מִזֶּה יוֹצֵא עִנְיַן אַזְהָרַת הַשִּׁיתּוּף וְהוּא מִפָּסוּק ה׳ אֶחָד כו׳.

---

27. A reference to *Sefer Hachinuch*, attributed by many to Rabbi Aaron Halevi of Barcelona (1230 – 1300). A disciple of the famed Ramban, he wrote novel Torah thoughts on the Talmud and halachic decisions. His more famous work is entitled *Bedek Habayit* where he counters the opinions of the Rashba. Rabbi Aaron's most renowned disciple was the Ritva.

28. Beginning with the premise that the Torah contains 613 commandments (248 positive and 365 negative), a number of sages have proposed enumerations of the commandments. These differ slightly in, among other things, determining which commandments of the Torah are to be counted as part of the 613. They also differ as to the exact source for each commandment in the verses of the Torah. In this case, the Rebbe cites three of the "enumerators," all of whom agree upon the source for the prohibition of *sheetuf*.

THE NUMERIC "ONE"

To understand this, one must understand the use of the word *echad* [one] in the context of the commandment to believe in G-d's Oneness. It would seem that the word *yachid* [Only, or Singular] would convey a stronger sense of exclusivity, since *echad* can also be used as a numeric "*one*" [i.e., one of many].

For example, despite the fact that there were 12 tribes of Israel, each one is called "one," as it is written, "send one of you"[29] or "one of your brothers,"[30] even though there was a second and a third. Or, for example, in the days of creation, which includes six days, yet the first one is called "one day," as it is written, "and it was evening and it was morning, one day."[31]

This is the concept of the "numeric *one*," which cannot, Heaven forbid, be used in reference to G-d. It would follow, then, that the expression "G-d is *Yachid*" would better convey the exclusivity of G-d's existence (see *Torah Or*[32] s.v. *Va'eira*.[33]) But since the verse that teaches us the commandment of His Unity contains the word *one*, it must give us a better understanding of the concept of G-d's exclusivity. But how?

ONE/EIGHT/FOUR

The matter is as follows. Our Sages say [regarding the meditation on the word *echad*]: "Once you [mentally] acknowledge Him as King above and below and to the four corners—nothing more is required."[34] This idea is hinted at in the word *echad*: the *chet* [numer-

---

29. Genesis 42:16.

30. Ibid. 42:19.

31. Genesis 1:5.

32. A collection of discourses elucidating major themes of the weekly Torah portion and Festivals according to Chasidic philosophy. Delivered by the founder of Chabad Chasidut, Rabbi Schneur Zalman of Liadi (1745 – 1812), they were published by his grandson Rabbi Menachem Mendel of Lubavitch, the Tzemach Tzedek (1789 – 1866).

33. 55b. In this *maamar*, Rabbi Schneur Zalman asks a similar question: "The term *Echad* (One) in the verse, "Hear, O Israel, the L-rd is our G-d, the L-rd [*Havayah*] is One," does not seem to express G-d's ultimate Oneness—that He is One and Only, and apart from Him there is nothing—because this term is also applied when counting. For example, Jacob bore twelve sons, yet Reuven is called number

וּלְהָבִין זֶה צָרִיךְ לְהָבִין מַה שֶּׁכָּתוּב בְּמִצְוַת לְיַיחֲדוֹ ה׳ אֶחָד, דִּלְכְאוֹרָה אִם הָיָה נֶאֱמַר יָחִיד הָיָה מוֹרֶה עַל אַחְדוּת יוֹתֵר, כִּי אֶחָד יֵשׁ גַּם אֶחָד הַמָּנוּי,

וְהַיְינוּ עַל דֶּרֶךְ מָשָׁל שִׁבְטֵי יִשְׂרָאֵל שֶׁהָיוּ י״ב וְאַף עַל פִּי כֵן נִקְרָא אֶחָד מֵהֶם בְּשֵׁם אֶחָד כְּמוֹ שֶׁכָּתוּב שִׁלְחוּ מִכֶּם אֶחָד אוֹ אֲחִיכֶם אֶחָד הֲגַם שֶׁיֵּשׁ שֵׁנִי וּשְׁלִישִׁי, אוֹ כְּמוֹ בְּשֵׁשֶׁת יְמֵי בְרֵאשִׁית שֶׁהֵם שֵׁשֶׁת יָמִים וְאַף עַל פִּי כֵן נִקְרָא הָרִאשׁוֹן אֶחָד כְּמוֹ שֶׁכָּתוּב וַיְהִי עֶרֶב וַיְהִי בֹקֶר יוֹם אֶחָד,

וְזֶהוּ עִנְיַן אֶחָד הַמָּנוּי מַה שֶּׁאִי אֶפְשָׁר חַס וְשָׁלוֹם לוֹמַר כֵּן בֶּאֱלֹקוּת, וְאִם כֵּן אִם הָיָה נֶאֱמַר ה׳ יָחִיד הָיָה מוֹרֶה יוֹתֵר עַל אַחְדוּתוֹ יִתְבָּרֵךְ, וְעַיֵּן בְּתוֹרָה־אוֹר בְּדִבּוּר הַמַּתְחִיל וָאֵרָא, וּמֵאַחַר שֶׁבַּפָּסוּק אֲשֶׁר לְמֵדִים מִמֶּנּוּ מִצְוַת לְיַיחֲדוֹ נֶאֱמַר דַּוְקָא אֶחָד מֵהַהֶכְרֵחַ לֵאמֹר שֶׁמִּתֵּיבַת אֶחָד אָנוּ יְכוֹלִים לְהָבִין יוֹתֵר עִנְיַן אַחְדוּתוֹ יִתְבָּרֵךְ וְצָרִיךְ לְהָבִין מַהוּ.

אַךְ הָעִנְיָן הוּא דְּהִנֵּה אָמְרוּ רַבּוֹתֵינוּ זִכְרוֹנָם לִבְרָכָה כַּד אַמְלִיכְתֵּיהּ לְמַעְלָה וּלְמַטָּה וּלְד׳ רוּחוֹת תּוּ לָא צְרִיכַת, וְזֶה

---

one (*echad*). Regarding Yitzchak however, [who was an only child,] the verse states, '*bincha yechidcha*' (your only son). Similarly, in reference to G-d, the term *Yachid* (Single) should be used."

Rabbi Schneur Zalman proceeds to explain that during the period of exile, G-d ascends to a plane that far transcends the world, and is unto Himself—Alone in His essence. His Oneness is not revealed in the lower worlds. Hence the verse, "on that day (i.e. in the future) G-d shall be One and His name One." During exile, while G-d is "hidden," the world seems to be a separate entity outside of G-d. Nevertheless, G-d gives us the ability to elicit His Oneness to a state of revelation within our multifarious world. This is the meaning of the verse, "Hear, O Israel": Israel must be aware that they are a people close to G-d, and therefore have the power to elicit the idea of *Havayah* to the lower worlds, that G-d's 'Oneness' be revealed *within* all the lower worlds.

34. *Berachot* 13b. The Talmud cites a Ba-

ically equivalent to eight[35]] alludes to the seven heavens[36] and the earth; the *dalet* [numerically equivalent to four] alludes to the four corners of the world. [The word *echad*, then, can be understood to mean that] although the seven heavens, the earth and the four corners of the world were created, [their existence does not contradict G-d's exclusivity because] they are entirely nullified to the "*alef*," which is the *Ein Sof*, the Master of the world Who creates them.

PUZZLING MIDRASH

[The following is] the explanation of the matter, to bring this idea—that the world and all its contents is nullified to the *Or Ein Sof* blessed be He—closer to the human mind. Our Sages state (*Pirkei d'Rabbi Eliezer*[37]):

> From what was the world created? —from the snow beneath the Throne of Glory. Land was formed from its dirt and mountains from its pebbles, as it is written (Job[38]), "He says to the snow: *Become earth!*"

Now the Sages' query regarding the origins of the earth seems puz-

---

raita that says, "whoever prolongs the pronunciation of the word *echad*, has his days and years prolonged." The Talmud then relates that Rabbi Yirmiyah prolonged his pronunciation of the word *echad* so much that he fell behind the congregation in prayer. (He would meditate on all the esoteric concepts alluded to in the word *echad.*) He was told by Rabbi Chiya bar Abba that while saying *echad* it was enough to merely acknowledge G-d's sovereignty over the heavens and earth and the four directions, this being the main idea alluded to in the word *echad* (as the Rebbe goes on to explain). See Maharsha *ad loc.*

35. Each of the 22 letters of the Hebrew alphabet has a numeric value. The first nine letters (א-ט) correspond to numbers 1–9 respectively. The next ten letters (י-צ) correspond to 10–90 respectively, while the last four letters (ק-ת) correspond to 100–400 respectively. See footnote 80.

36. See *Chagigah* 12b. "Rabbi Yehudah stated: 'There are two heavens, as it is written (Deut. 10:14), 'The heaven, the heaven of heaven, the earth and everything in it, all belong to G-d.' Reish Lakish maintains there are seven heavens, namely: *Vilon* ("Curtain"), *Rakiya* ("Sky"), *Sh'chakim* ("Mills"), *Z'vul* ("Residence"), *Ma'on* ("Abode"), *Machon* ("Arsenal") and *Aravot* ("Plains," or "Wide Spaces")." Rambam (*Yesodei Hatorah* 3:1) refers to *Shamayim*, the heavens, as *Galgalim*, spheres. *Kesef Mishnah* explains: "Rabbi Yehudah and Reish Lakish do not disagree; rather, Rabbi Yehudah counts the visible heavens only (the *Shamayim*), whereas Reish Lakish also counts the celestial aspects—which are loftier than *Shamayim*—and calls them all *Shamayim*. As

מְרוּמָּז בְּתֵיבַת אֶחָד שֶׁהַחֵי״ת רוֹמֵז לְז׳ רְקִיעִים וָאֶרֶץ וְהַדַּלֵי״ת רוֹמֵז לְד׳ רוּחוֹת הָעוֹלָם, וְהַיְינוּ כִּי הֲגַם שֶׁנִּתְהַווּ ז׳ רְקִיעִים וָאָרֶץ וְד׳ רוּחוֹת הָעוֹלָם עִם כָּל זֶה הֵם בְּטֵלִים בְּתַכְלִית לִבְחִינַת אָלֶ״ף הוּא בְּחִינַת אֵין סוֹף אַלּוּפוֹ שֶׁל עוֹלָם הַמְהַוָּום כו׳.

וּבֵיאוּר הָעִנְיָן לְקָרֵב אֶל הַשֵּׂכֶל אֵיךְ הָעוֹלָם וּמְלוֹאָהּ בָּטֵל לְגַבֵּי אוֹר אֵין סוֹף בָּרוּךְ הוּא, הִנֵּה אָמְרוּ רַבּוֹתֵינוּ זִכְרוֹנָם לִבְרָכָה בְּפִרְקֵי דְרַבִּי אֱלִיעֶזֶר

הָאָרֶץ מֵהֵיכָן נִבְרֵאת מִשֶּׁלֶג שֶׁתַּחַת כִּסֵּא הַכָּבוֹד, מֵעָפָר שֶׁבָּהּ נַעֲשָׂה אֶרֶץ, וּמִצְּרוֹרִים שֶׁבָּהּ נַעֲשָׂה הָרִים שֶׁנֶּאֱמַר כִּי לַשֶּׁלֶג אָמַר הֱוֵי אָרֶץ (בְּאִיּוֹב).

וְלִכְאוֹרָה צָרִיךְ לְהָבִין מַה הַחֲקִירָה אֶרֶץ מֵהֵיכָן נִבְרֵאת,

---

Reish Lakish continues to enumerate (*Chagigah* ibid.): *Vilon* serves no purpose. *Rakiyah* contains the sun, moon, stars, zodiac and all the Heavenly Hosts. In *Sh'chakim*, the mills grind manna for the Righteous for the World to Come. *Z'vul* contains an altar upon which the angel Michael, the great minister, offers sacrifices. In *Ma'on*, groups of angels chant song. *Machon* contains storages of snow and hail. *Aravot* contains righteousness and justice, the vaults of life and peace and the vaults of blessing, the souls of the righteous, spirits and souls to be born in the future and the dew with which G-d will resurrect the dead. So it has been explained that all the objects in the higher five heavens are not physical objects at all. The terms "snow," "hail" and "dew" are all metaphors for the beneficience which descends from above." Rabbi Yehudah only counts the lower two heavens, visible to the physical eye, containing objects such as the sun, moon and stars.

37. Chap. 3. *Pirkei d'Rabbi Eliezer* is a *Midrash* authored by the second century Mishnaic Sage, Rabbi Eliezer ben Horkenus, also known as Rabbi Eliezer Hagadol ("the great"). "The earliest of all Tannaic treatises, revealed and famous in the era of our authoritative Rabbis and mystical Kabbalists, the *Rishonim*, who used and benefited from its light" (from the title page).

38. 37:6. Literally, the verse means that at the appropriate season, G-d commands the snow to fall to the earth. *Pirkei d'Rabbi Eliezer* translates the verse metaphorically that snow refers to the *Galgalim* (spheres), beneath the Throne of Glory. In Creation, G-d tells this "snow" to actually become earth.

zling, since the earth was created *ex nihilo*. Even the philosophers agree to this, as Rasag[39] writes regarding Creation, that being was created from non-being.[40] So what is the meaning of the question: "From what was it created?"

A similar query is found in *Midrash Rabbah*,[41] where our Sages say:

> From where was the light created? This teaches that G-d cloaked Himself in a white *tallit*, and radiated the brilliance of His glory.

This query is puzzling as well. Why inquire about the origin of light when it was in fact created *ex nihilo* by the Divine utterance of *Let there be light!*—one of the Ten Utterances [with which the world was created[42]]?

The matter is as follows. For every minute part of all physical creatures there is a spiritual root and source. As our Sages say: "There is no [blade of] grass below that does not have a *mazal* above that strikes it and says to it, 'Grow!'" [43]

MAZAL

Mazal is the root and source [of a thing. In this case it refers to the root of] vegetation and grass that grows in the physical world. Indeed in a loftier form, these are angels, which are called vegetation and grass, or foliage and grass. As stated in *Zohar*[44] regarding the verse,[45] "He causes foliage to sprout for the animal and grass through the work of man." These are two levels of angels, who are referred to in the phrase "Creator of ministering angels,"[46] since they sing praise each day and are subsumed and nullified within the

---

39. Acronym for Rabbi Saadiah Gaon (892 – 942 CE). Born in the ancient city of Pitom in Egypt, he was one of the greatest leaders of Jewry in his time. He authored an Arabic commentary on (apparently) the entire Scripture. He was a profound Kabbalist and a prolific writer, and also arranged a prayer book including liturgical hymns, laws, confession prayers for the yearly cycle and an enumeration of the 613 Mitzvot.

40. *Emunot V'deiot* 1. The same is written in *The Guide for the Perplexed* (1:13) (fn. on *Mayim Rabim 5636*).

41. A major collection of homilies and commentaries on the Torah, attributed to Rabbi Oshaya Rabbah (circa. 3rd century); some place it as a work of the early Gaonic period.

42. Genesis 1:3. The world was created by

הֲלֹא הִיא נִבְרֵאת מֵאַיִן לְיֵשׁ, וַאֲפִילוּ הַחוֹקְרִים מוֹדִים בָּזֶה וּכְמוֹ שֶׁכָּתַב הָרְסַ״ג בְּעִנְיַן הַבְּרִיאָה שֶׁנִּבְרָא דָבָר מִלֹּא דָבָר, וּמַה עִנְיַן הַשְּׁאֵלָה מֵהֵיכָן נִבְרֵאת.

וְעַל דֶּרֶךְ זֶה יֵשׁ בְּמִדְרָשׁ רַבָּה גַם כֵּן שֶׁאָמְרוּ רַבּוֹתֵינוּ זִכְרוֹנָם לִבְרָכָה

הָאוֹרָה מֵהֵיכָן נִבְרֵאת מְלַמֵּד שֶׁנִּתְעַטֵּף הַקָּדוֹשׁ בָּרוּךְ הוּא בְּטַלִּית לְבָנָה וְהִבְהִיק זִיו הֲדָרוֹ,

שֶׁגַּם בָּזֶה צָרִיךְ לְהָבִין כַּנַ״ל מַה הַשְּׁאֵלָה מֵהֵיכָן נִבְרָא, שֶׁנִּבְרָא יֵשׁ מֵאַיִן מִמַּאֲמַר יְהִי אוֹר שֶׁבַּעֲשָׂרָה מַאֲמָרוֹת.

אַךְ הָעִנְיָן הוּא שֶׁלְּכָל דָּבָר וְדָבָר שֶׁבִּפְרָטֵי גַשְׁמִיּוּת הַנִּבְרָאִים יֵשׁ שׁוֹרֶשׁ וּמָקוֹר בְּרוּחָנִיּוּת, וּכְמַאֲמַר רַבּוֹתֵינוּ זִכְרוֹנָם לִבְרָכָה אֵין לְךָ עֵשֶׂב מִלְּמַטָּה שֶׁאֵין לוֹ מַזָּל מִלְמַעְלָה הַמַּכֶּה בּוֹ וְאוֹמֵר לוֹ גְּדַל

שֶׁעִנְיַן הַמַּזָּל הוּא שׁוֹרֶשׁ וּמְקוֹר הַדֶּשֶׁא וְהָעֵשֶׂב הַצּוֹמֵחַ לְמַטָּה עַד שֶׁגָּבוֹהַּ מֵעַל גָּבוֹהַּ הֵם הַמַּלְאָכִים שֶׁנִּקְרָאִים בְּשֵׁם דֶּשֶׁא וְעֵשֶׂב אוֹ חָצִיר וְעֵשֶׂב וּכְמוֹ שֶׁכָּתוּב בְּזֹהַר בְּעִנְיַן מַצְמִיחַ חָצִיר לַבְּהֵמָה וְעֵשֶׂב לַעֲבוֹדַת הָאָדָם, וְהֵם הַמַּלְאָכִים שֶׁנִּקְרָאִים בְּשֵׁם יוֹצֵר מְשָׁרְתִים שֶׁאוֹמְרִים שִׁירָה בְּכָל יוֹם

---

means of ten Divine utterances (*Avot* 5:1). In the account of Creation, the words "And G-d said, Let…" occur nine times, one of which is: "And G-d said, Let there be light." The first word of Genesis, "In the beginning," indicates the first of the Divine Utterances, which created the heavens, as it is written (Psalms 33:6), "By the word of G-d were the heavens made." The Rebbe is therefore puzzled by the inquiry in *Pirkei d'Rabbi Eliezer*, "From where was the light created."

43. *Bereishit Rabbah* 10:7; *Zohar* I, Supplements 251a; II:171a.

44. *Zohar* I:18b – 19b. See footnote 47.

45. Psalms 104:14.

46. Liturgy, Morning Prayer, *Siddur Tehilat Hashem* p. 43.

ayin[47] [the "nothingness" of Divinity[48]], and "His ministering angels," who have been standing at the height of the universe since the six days of creation, as has been explained elsewhere.[49]

TALKING FLORA

With this we can understand a saying of our Sages (*Chulin*[50]):

> The plants applied a *kal v'chomer* ["*a fortiori* logic"] to themselves: "If regarding trees, which do not grow commingled, the verse states 'to their kind,'[51]—we, who grow commingled, certainly [should take care not to crossbreed]!"

Now, how could plants, of the vegetable kingdom, have "stated" a *kal v'chomer*? Where did they derive the power of speech and intellect to state a *kal v'chomer*? The answer is that it is not the grass or plant that states the *kal v'chomer*, but its spiritual root and origin. This root is the *mazal*, which manifests on loftier and loftier levels as far as its manifestation as the supernal angels. These angels have the power of speech, they sing praise, and they are capable of formulating a *kal v'chomer*.

In spite of their superiority, they serve as the origins of plant life, since they are the primary manifestation of supernal emotions, which [like plant life,] experience growth from smallness to greatness[52]:

---

47. The *Zohar* (ibid.) states that "foliage" refers to angels that must be recreated each day, since they repeatedly escape their existence. However, the second half of the verse, "grass," refers to the "ministering angles"—*serafim*, *ofanim* and *chayot*—who endure in their existence because they are designed for the upkeep of the world and mankind. These are called "grass." This is discussed at length in *Or Hatorah*, *Bereishit* 33b ff. and *Likkutei Torah*, *Pinchas* 79b ff. See also *Likkutei Torah*, *Emor* 36a, *Haazinu* 76d; *Maamarim 5661* p. 207 ff.

48. It is called "nothing" because it is not perceivable by the created being.

49. The *maamar* refers here to a *maamar* of the same year entitled *Seh Tamim*, where he expounds on the aforementioned passage of the *Zohar*. See fn. 47.

50. 60a.

51. Cf. Genesis 1:11.

52. There are four elements or grades with which the world was created: Mineral (*domem*, "silent"), Vegetable (*tzomeach*, "that which grows"), Animal (*chai*, "alive") and Man (*medaber*, "one that can speak"). These four elements correspond to the four letters of G-d's Name, *Havayah* (see fn. 123): the first letter, *Yud*, corresponds to Human, *Hey* to Animal, *Vav* to Vegetable, and the second *Hey* to Mineral. In

וְנִכְלָלִים וְנִבְטָלִים לְאַיִן, וַאֲשֶׁר מְשָׁרְתָיו שֶׁעוֹמְדִים בְּרוּם עוֹלָם מִשֵּׁשֶׁת יְמֵי בְרֵאשִׁית, כְּמוֹ שֶׁכָּתוּב בְּמָקוֹם אַחֵר,

וּבָזֶה יוּבַן מַאֲמַר רַבּוֹתֵינוּ זִכְרוֹנָם לִבְרָכָה בְּחוּלִּין

שֶׁנָּשְׂאוּ דְשָׁאִים קַל וָחֹמֶר בְּעַצְמָם וּמָה אִילָנוֹת שֶׁאֵין דַּרְכָּם לָצֵאת בְּעִרְבּוּבְיָא אָמַר הַכָּתוּב לְמִינֵיהֶם אָנוּ שֶׁדַּרְכֵּינוּ לָצֵאת בְּעִרְבּוּבְיָא עַל אַחַת כַּמָּה וְכַמָּה,

שֶׁלִּכְאוֹרָה יִפָּלֵא אֵיךְ יִשְׂאוּ דְשָׁאִים קַל וָחֹמֶר בְּעַצְמָם הֲלֹא הֵם צוֹמֵחַ וְאֵיךְ יִהְיֶה בָּהֶם הַדִּבּוּר וְהַשֵּׂכֶל לֵאמֹר קַל וָחֹמֶר כו׳. אַךְ הָעִנְיָן הוּא שֶׁאֵין הַדֶּשֶׁא וְהָעֵשֶׂב אוֹמֵר הַקַּל וָחֹמֶר כִּי אִם שָׁרְשׁוֹ וּמְקוֹרוֹ בְּרוּחָנִיּוּת שֶׁהוּא בְּחִינַת הַמַּזָּל שֶׁגָּבוֹהַּ מֵעַל גָּבוֹהַּ עַד הַמַּלְאָכִים הָעֶלְיוֹנִים שֶׁיֵּשׁ בָּהֶם הַדִּבּוּר שֶׁאוֹמְרִים שִׁירָה וְהֵם יְכוֹלִים גַּם כֵּן לָשֵׂאת קַל וָחֹמֶר

וְעִם כָּל זֶה הֵם מְקוֹרִים עַל בְּחִינַת הַצּוֹמֵחַ לִהְיוֹת כִּי בָּהֶם הוּא עִיקַר בְּחִינַת הַמִּדּוֹת שֶׁהֵם בִּבְחִינַת צְמִיחָה קַטְנוּת

---

sefirot, Man is *chochmah*, Animal is *binah*, Vegetable is *chesed* through *yesod* (the six emotions), and Mineral is *malchut*. In addition, the four letters of *Havayah* correspond to the four major divisions of the *sefirot: Yud – chochmah*, *Hey – binah*, *Vav* – the first six "emotions" (*chesed* through *yesod*), and *Hey – malchut*. Hence, the six emotions correspond to Vegetable/ Growth.

In human terms, Mineral corresponds to thought, speech and action, which are "inanimate" and, unlike emotion or intellect, are unable to produce additional thought, speech and action. They are also compared to the letters of speech and thought, which are "inanimate" vessels for the ideas and feelings they contain. (*Sefer Yetzirah* calls letters "stones.") Vegetable/ Growth corresponds to emotions—love, fear etc.—which experience "growth," i.e., maturation, as the person matures. They also "grow" in intensity as one ponders and contemplates the beauty and desirability of a thing, or, conversely, the destructiveness and repulsiveness of a thing. The angels also are described as grass, i.e., Vegetable, since they experience emotion—love and awe of G-d. They also experience growth, i.e., their stature increases when they are engaged in song or the fulfillment of some mission. Animal, or *Chai* (translated not as animal but as "alive") corresponds to intellect, which "gives life to all that possess it" (Ecclesiastes 7:12). (See *Likkutei Torah, Chukat* 58a; *Torat Chaim* pp. 19d – 22b.)

Man, unique in his ability to speak,

from before the fulfillment of their mission to during the mission, and from before their song to during their song.

NAMELESS MESSENGERS

Their growth and added stature is so great that, while fulfilling their mission, angels can call themselves by the Name of G-d. Thus it is written,[53] "And [the angel] said [to Abraham], 'I have sworn by Myself, says G-d…'"[54] It is also written, "[Hagar] gave a name to G-d who had spoken to her…"[55] This is because the angel is entirely nullified while fulfilling his mission, so much so that he identifies himself by the name of the One who sends him. For his being is completely nullified and his entire existence is the power of his appointment [as G-d's agent].

[Thus the angels, who experience various measures of being] are similar to plants, which grow from small to large. Hence the angels—although possessed of the power of speech etc.—are the roots for plant life, since their primary characteristic is emotion.

This, is the meaning of a statement of our Sages (*Midrash Rabbah, parshat Terumah*[56]):

> Everything that exists Above exists Below: Above stand *serafs*,[57] and Below stand cedar trees.[58]

It is also written, "Then all the trees of the forest will sing,"[59] referring to the angels that are called "trees of the forest," so named because they are the source and origin of vegetation, the trees and plants of earth.

THE ROOSTER

As it is with plant life—grass, flora, trees—so it is with all the elements—mineral, vegetable, animal, human—which were created

---

corresponds to *Keter* (Crown), the essence of the soul, whence the ability to speak—and thus the letters and words of speech—stem. (For it is speech whose entire being exists solely for the other, so that one can communicate to others. And it is in "leaving" itself and serving others that the soul's essence and infinity is expressed. As long as it is self-contained, even in the loftiest thoughts, it has not transcended its limited self. Thus Man is referred to by his ability to speak (*medaber*), not his ability to think.)

53. Genesis 22:16.

54. In this verse the angel refers to himself as G-d.

וְגַדְלוּת, וּמִקּוֹדֶם הַשְּׁלִיחוּת לְשַׁעַת הַשְּׁלִיחוּת, אוֹ מִקּוֹדֶם הַשִּׁירָה לְשַׁעַת הַשִּׁירָה

שֶׁהַצְּמִיחָה וְהַתּוֹסֶפֶת הִיא בְּהַגְדָּלָה בְּתוֹסֶפֶת וְרִיבּוּי, עַד כִּי בְּשַׁעַת הַשְּׁלִיחוּת יָכוֹל הַמַּלְאָךְ לִקְרוֹא אֶת עַצְמוֹ בְּשֵׁם ה׳ כְּמוֹ שֶׁכָּתוּב וַיֹּאמֶר בִּי נִשְׁבַּעְתִּי נְאוּם הוי׳ וּכְתִיב וַתִּקְרָא שֵׁם ה׳ הַדּוֹבֵר אֵלֶיהָ, וְהַיְינוּ לְפִי שֶׁבְּעֵת הַשְּׁלִיחוּת הוּא בָּטֵל לְגַמְרֵי עַד שֶׁקּוֹרֵא לְעַצְמוֹ עַל שֵׁם הַמְשַׁלֵּחַ לְפִי שֶׁמִּתְבַּטֵּל כָּל מַהוּתוֹ לְגַמְרֵי שֶׁאֵין בּוֹ רַק כֹּחַ הַשְּׁלִיחוּת כו׳

וַהֲרֵי זֶה כְּמָשָׁל הַצּוֹמֵחַ שֶׁמִּשְׁתַּנֶּה מִקַּטְנוּת לְגַדְלוּת כו׳, וְלָכֵן הֵם מְקוֹרִים עַל בְּחִינַת הַצּוֹמֵחַ הֲגַם כִּי יֵשׁ בָּהֶם הַדִּיבּוּר גַּם כֵּן כו׳ עִם כָּל זֶה הָעִיקָּר הוּא הַמִּדָּה כו׳.

וְזֶהוּ שֶׁאָמְרוּ רַבּוֹתֵינוּ זִכְרוֹנָם לִבְרָכָה בְּמִדְרָשׁ רַבָּה פָּרָשַׁת תְּרוּמָה

שֶׁכָּל מַה שֶּׁיֵּשׁ לְמַעְלָה יֵשׁ לְמַטָּה, לְמַעְלָה שְׂרָפִים עוֹמְדִים וּלְמַטָּה עֲצֵי שִׁטִּים עוֹמְדִים,

וּכְתִיב אָז יְרַנְּנוּ כָּל עֲצֵי הַיָּעַר שֶׁקָּאֵי עַל הַמַּלְאָכִים שֶׁנִּקְרָאִים בְּשֵׁם עֲצֵי הַיָּעַר, וְהַיְינוּ לִהְיוֹתָם מְקוֹרִים וְשָׁרָשִׁים לִבְחִינַת הַצּוֹמֵחַ אִילָנוֹת וּדְשָׁאִים שֶׁלְּמַטָּה כו׳.

וּכְמוֹ שֶׁהוּא בְּמִין הַצּוֹמֵחַ דֶּשֶׁא וְעֵשֶׂב וְאִילָנוֹת כְּמוֹ כֵן הוּא

---

55. Genesis 16:13, again referring to an angel.

56. 35:6.

57. Cf. Isaiah 6:2.

58. Exodus 26:15. Angels exist primarily in the world of *Yetzirah*, which is called, "the World of Angels." *Serafim* exist in the world of *Beriah*, and hence, are loftier than the angels of *Yetzirah* and *Asiyah*. Similarly, cedar trees grow higher than other trees. Therefore, the loftiest angels are compared to cedar trees (*Maamarim 5630* p.94). See also fn. 47.

59. Psalms 96:12.

during the six days of creation. As our Sages say, "When the rooster crows, one recites the blessing, "[Blessed are You G-d...] who grants the rooster understanding [to distinguish between day and night]."[60] Now, at first glance, it is not clear why the blessing regarding the rooster's understanding is recited specifically when the rooster crows and not earlier. What connection is there between the meaning of the blessing to the rooster's crow?[61]

FOUR WORLDS

The explanation is that on the physical plane, we perceive a rooster; but on a higher plane, in the source of its source in the world of *Yetzirah*,[62] it is the angel Gabriel.[63]

And in Atzilut, its source is the five attributes of severity of *binah* that awaken *malchut* from its descent into *B'ya* [*Beriah, Yetzirah, Assiyah*] each night[64]—as it is written: "she rises when it is still night and gives food to her household...."[65] At midnight, the five attributes of severity of *binah* awaken *malchut* from its descent into *B'ya* and raise it to *Atzilut* etc., as known.

---

60. *Berachot* 60b. See also *Siddur Tehilat Hashem* p. 7.

61. In the words of Rosh (*Berachot*, ibid), "one who did not hear the rooster's crow can make this blessing, which is merely to thank G-d who gave us understanding and created all our needs for us." If the blessing is merely to thank G-d for creating all our needs, why must it be recited at the actual time of the rooster's crow? Can we not thank G-d at *anytime* for creating all our needs? (See also *Sefer Hamaamarim 5711* p. 8.)

62. THE FOUR WORLDS: Kabbalah and *Chasidut* explain the phenomenon of the creation of a finite physical universe by an Infinite Creator with the concept of *tzimtzum*, contraction and concealment. G-d effected a series of concealments of His presence and infinitude, resulting ultimately, in the creation of our physical universe, through virtually total concealment of G-d. The non-corporeal intermediate steps between the Creator and this material world are called "Worlds," referring to the basic levels of spiritual existence in the creative process. The differentiation reflects their level of concealment of the Divine Light, the higher worlds receiving in a more revealed form.

In general, there are Four Worlds: *Atzilut* (World of Emanation—a state of proximity and relative unity with G-d); *Beriah* (World of Creation); *Yetzirah* (World of Formation); *Asiyah* (World of Action or Making—the final stage in the creative process). The four worlds have been compared to the elements inherent to building a house. Four stages are necessary: 1) A general idea, as yet undefined; 2) A definite idea of the house in one's mind, 3) The architectural plan or design; 4) The

בְּכָל פְּרָטֵי דְבָרִים דוֹמֵם־צוֹמֵחַ־חַי־מְדַבֵּר שֶׁנִּתְהַווּ בְּמַעֲשֵׂה בְרֵאשִׁית, וּכְמַאֲמַר רַבּוֹתֵינוּ זִכְרוֹנָם לִבְרָכָה כַּד קָארֵי תַּרְנְגוֹלְתָּא מְבָרֵךְ הַנּוֹתֵן לַשֶּׂכְוִי בִינָה, שֶׁלִּכְאוֹרָה אֵינוֹ מוּבָן מַה שַּׁיָּיכוּת עִנְיַן בִּרְכַּת הַנּוֹתֵן לַשֶּׂכְוִי בִּינָה לִקְרִיאַת הַתַּרְנְגוֹל דַּוְקָא, שֶׁכַּאֲשֶׁר קוֹרֵא אָז חִיּוּב הַבְּרָכָה וְלֹא קוֹדֶם לָכֵן,

אַךְ הָעִנְיָן הוּא דְּמַה שֶּׁלְּמַטָּה הוּא תַּרְנְגוֹל לְמַעְלָה בְּשׁוֹרֶשׁ שָׁרְשׁוֹ בִּיצִירָה הוּא מַלְאָךְ גַּבְרִיאֵל

וּבְשָׁרְשׁוֹ בַּאֲצִילוּת הוּא בְּחִינַת ה׳ גְבוּרוֹת דְּבִינָה שֶׁמְּעוֹרְרִים בְּחִינַת הַמַּלְכוּת מִירִידָתָהּ בִּבְרִיאָה־יְצִירָה־עֲשִׂיָּה בְּכָל לַיְלָה, כְּמוֹ שֶׁכָּתוּב וַתָּקָם בְּעוֹד לַיְלָה וַתִּתֵּן טֶרֶף לְבֵיתָהּ וּבַחֲצוֹת לַיְלָה מְעוֹרְרִים ה׳ גְבוּרוֹת דְּבִינָה אֶת הַמַּלְכוּת מִירִידָתָהּ בִּבְרִיאָה־יְצִירָה־עֲשִׂיָּה לְהִתְעַלּוֹת בַּאֲצִילוּת כו׳ כְּנוֹדָע,

---

actual building of the house (*Tanya*, Bi-Lingual Edition, Kehot 1998, p. 844).

"Higher" (or "Supernal") and "Lower" refer to stages closer or more distant from the Creator, with a greater or lesser awareness of Him (not, of course, implying physical distance). Lower Worlds appear to be independent entities from the Creator.

Through the performance of *mitzvot* and subordination of the physical world to the Divine purpose, all Worlds are elevated, and experience a clearer apprehension of G-d. See *Mystical Concepts in Chassidism*, ch. 2 (*Tzimtzum*) and ch. 4 (Worlds).

63. See footnote 58.

64. The crowing of the rooster at dawn is the physical manifestation of the call of Gabriel to awaken the souls in Gan Eden, as explained below. On a higher plane though, there must also be some sort of "awakening." This is *binah* awakening *malchut* from its major descent. See next footnote.

65. Proverbs 31:15. *Malchut* of *Atzilut*, is the recipient of G-dly influx in order to pass it on to Creation. However, since it is impossible to be a recipient and an emanator simultaneously, therefore, during the day, *malchut* receives the influx from *Atzilut* and internalizes it. At night, *malchut* lowers herself to "give food," i.e., the influx, to the lower worlds. But at midnight, the point when the night begins to turn into day, the influx is withheld as the five attributes of severity of *binah* awaken *malchut* from its descent into the three lower worlds and raise it back to its source in *Atzilut*, and the process is repeated. (*Maamarei Admur Hazaken 5562*, vol. 2 p. 395 ff.)

Similarly in the case of the creatures of *B'ya*: "at midnight, the Holy One blessed be He comes to delight in the righteous of the Garden of Eden."[66] Therefore, the angel Gabriel awakens the souls so that they can delight in and benefit from the splendor of the *Shechinah* [that shines] in the lower Garden of Eden and the higher one, etc.[67]

And in this world at midnight, one must arise and praise [G-d], as David says: "At midnight I arise to praise You...."[68] It is then that the rooster, whose source is from the level of Gabriel, calls out to awaken man to arise at midnight. As the *Zohar* states, the rooster does not crow willingly. Rather, there are two flames of fire burning beneath its wings,[69] which cause it to crow, as a person screams when being hit.

So the blessing for the rooster's understanding refers to its root and source in *binah* of *Atzilut*, or *malchut* of *Atzilut*. (See the discourse entitled *Yafah sha'ah achat biteshuvah umaasim tovim b'olam hazeh 5629*, regarding the concept of "*chai chai yoducha komoni*.")[70]

Therefore, the appropriate time for the blessing is specifically when the rooster crows, since it crows when the five attributes of severity are awakened [in *Atzilut*]; and in *B'ya* at that time, Gabriel awakens the righteous; and on the earthly plane, the rooster crows to

---

66. *Zohar* I:92b. "Play," i.e., to delight with.

67. At midnight, G-d remembers the destruction of the *Beit Hamikdash* and mourns it. However, He is "comforted" by the Torah study of the righteous, and thus delights with them. In doing so, the *Shechinah* shines in the Garden of Eden, where the souls of the righteous are located. Man, i.e., the righteous, was placed in the Garden of Eden "to work it and guard it" (Genesis 2:15). This means that the primary purpose of man's creation is to "labor at the Garden of Eden," i.e., to elicit a revelation of G-dliness into this world. The term *Shechinah* refers to a revelation of G-dliness to create all the worlds. Thus, because man, i.e. the righteous, reveals G-dliness, the *Shechinah* delights. This takes place at midnight as midnight is the time when *malchut* begins its elevation back to its source and by doing so casts off its "worldly" concealment, becoming revealed once again; it is uplifted by the midnight Torah study of the righteous (*Likkutei Torah*, *Shir Hashirim* 31d).

68. Psalms 119:62.

69. This expression is quoted several times

וְעַל דֶּרֶךְ זֶה בַּנִּבְרָאִים דִּבְרִיאָה־יְצִירָה־עֲשִׂיָּה, הִנֵּה בַּחֲצוֹת לַיְלָה קוּדְשָׁא בְּרִיךְ הוּא אָתֵי לְאִשְׁתַּעֲשְׁעָא עִם צַדִּיקַיָּיא בְּגִינְתָא דְעֵדֶן, לָכֵן מַלְאָךְ גַּבְרִיאֵל מְעוֹרֵר הַנְּשָׁמוֹת שֶׁיִּתְעַנְּגוּ וְיֵהָנוּ מִזִּיו הַשְּׁכִינָה שֶׁבְּגַן עֵדֶן הַתַּחְתּוֹן וְהָעֶלְיוֹן כו',

וּכְמוֹ כֵן בָּעוֹלָם הַזֶּה הִנֵּה בַּחֲצוֹת הַלַּיְלָה צָרִיךְ לָקוּם לְהוֹדוֹת כְּמוֹ שֶׁאָמַר דָּוִד חֲצוֹת לַיְלָה אָקוּם לְהוֹדוֹת לָךְ כו', אָז קוֹרֵא הַתַּרְנְגוֹל שֶׁשָּׁרְשׁוֹ מִבְּחִינַת גַּבְרִיאֵל לְעוֹרֵר אֶת הָאָדָם שֶׁיָּקוּם בַּחֲצוֹת הַלַּיְלָה, וּכְמוֹ שֶׁכָּתוּב בְּזֹהַר שֶׁהַתַּרְנְגוֹל קוֹרֵא שֶׁלֹּא בְּטוֹבָתוֹ, לִהְיוֹת כִּי תְּרֵין שַׁלְהוֹבִין דְּנוּרָא מְקוֹדִין לֵיהּ תְּחוֹת גַּדְפַּיָּא, שֶׁקּוֹרֵא מֵחֲמַת זֶה בְּהֶכְרֵחַ כְּמוֹ הָאָדָם שֶׁצּוֹעֵק כְּשֶׁמַּכִּין אוֹתוֹ כו',

וְנִמְצָא כִּי בִּרְכַּת הַנּוֹתֵן לַשֶּׂכְוִי בִינָה הִיא עַל שׁוֹרֶשׁ וּמָקוֹר שֶׁבַּאֲצִילוּת בְּבִינָה אוֹ בְּמַלְכוּת דַּאֲצִילוּת עַיֵּן בְּדִבּוּר הַמַּתְחִיל יָפָה שָׁעָה אַחַת בִּתְשׁוּבָה וּמַעֲשִׂים טוֹבִים בָּעוֹלָם הַזֶּה (ר"ט), בְּעִנְיַן חַי חַי יוֹדְךָ כָּמוֹנִי,

הִנֵּה זְמַן בְּרָכָה זוֹ הוּא דַּוְקָא בִּזְמַן קְרִיאַת הַתַּרְנְגוֹל לִהְיוֹת כִּי זְמַן קְרִיאָתוֹ הוּא בִּזְמַן הַהִתְעוֹרְרוּת דְּה' גְבוּרוֹת דְּבִינָה,

---

in Chasidic literature. However, references are made to different sources each time. Perhaps this is because the entire passage is apparently not stated in full as quoted. *Or Hatorah*, *Massei* p. 1395 traces it to *Zohar* III:107a ff. In *Mayim Rabbim 5636*, the Rebbe locates it in *Zohar* I:77b and I:218b noting, "This needs clarification since these sources say that only one flame burns beneath its wings." In *Sefer Hamaamarim 5711* p. 14, the Rebbe makes reference to *Zohar* II:196a, III:22b and III:171b.

Fire burns beneath the rooster's wings to cause it to crow, which results in the crowing of the physical rooster, thus awakening us to praise G-d.

70. The *maamar* now provides the answer to why the blessing of the rooster must be recited exactly at the proper time. The blessing actually elicits the entire process of "awakening," beginning with the five severities of *binah* awakening *malchut*, continuing with the angel Gabriel awakening the souls in *Gan Eden* and finally the physical rooster awakening mankind from sleep.

Indeed each one of the Morning Blessings elicits G-d's Light to oversee the world and infuse it with energy. See *Sefer Hamaamarim 5629* (p. 44) for an elaboration of this concept.

awaken us from our sleep so that we should rise at midnight and praise [G-d]. So precisely that moment is the proper time for the blessing.

EVOLVEMENT

Now when one contemplates the myriad stages that must exist so that a physical rooster can evolve[71] and emerge from the angel Gabriel [one recognizes that physical matter is merely a devolved form of a far loftier entity.]

Consider: The angels are the greatest beings of all those created during the six days of creation. Of them David said: "How great are Your works, O G-d!"[72] As is known, there is a difference between the phrase "How manifold"[73] and "How great." *How manifold* refers to the particulars of the creatures of the four elements: mineral, vegetable, animal, and human. *How great*, by contrast, refers to the great [and awesome] creatures (as explained in the *maamar* entitled *Mi yitencha*,[74] and in the explanation and notes there. See also *Likutei Torah*, *Shir Hashirim*, s.v. *Yonati b'chagvei*, regarding the angels—that an angel occupies up a third of the world[75] etc.).

So for a physical rooster to evolve from the angel Gabriel, there must be myriad stages of evolvement in between. Similarly, every spiritual entity must descend through myriad stages of evolvement before becoming a source for a physical entity.

YESH ME'AYIN

Now, the evolvement [of a spiritual entity] alone could not create a physical being, for it would remain in the realm of the spiritual. Even myriad stages of evolvement could not create physicality from spirit. It would remain spirit. Physicality can only come into ex-

---

71. "Evolve" generally connotes an upward progression and development. In this case we are using the word in the context of a downward progression. I.e., an entity starts out as a spiritual being and "evolves"—actually "devolves"—to a point where it is a coarsened physical being. See fn. 86.

72. Psalms 92:6.

73. Psalms 104:24.

74. *Likkutei Torah*, *Shir Hashirim* 44c; *Or Hatorah*, *Shir Hashirim* pp. 636, 652, 676. See also *Sefer Hamaamarim 5626* p. 105.

וּבִבְרִיאָה־יְצִירָה־עֲשִׂיָּה אָז זְמַן שֶׁגַּבְרִיאֵל מְעוֹרֵר הַצַּדִּיקִים, וּלְמַטָּה בִּכְדֵי שֶׁיָּקוּם בַּחֲצוֹת הַלַּיְלָה לְהוֹדוֹת קוֹרֵא אָז הַתַּרְנְגוֹל לְעוֹרֵר אוֹתָנוּ מִן הַשֵּׁינָה, לָכֵן אָז דַּוְקָא הַזְּמַן שֶׁשַּׁיָּיךְ בְּרָכָה זוֹ.

וְהִנֵּה כְּשֶׁיִּתְבּוֹנֵן כַּמָּה רִבְבוֹת מַדְרֵגוֹת צְרִיכוֹת לִהְיוֹת דֶּרֶךְ הִשְׁתַּלְשְׁלוּת עַד שֶׁיִּהְיֶה יָכוֹל לִהְיוֹת וּלְהִשְׁתַּלְשֵׁל מִן מַלְאָךְ גַּבְרִיאֵל בְּחִינַת הַתַּרְנְגוֹל הַגַּשְׁמִי,

שֶׁהֲרֵי הַמַּלְאָכִים הֵם הַנִּבְרָאִים הַגְּדוֹלִים שֶׁבְּמַעֲשֵׂה בְרֵאשִׁית שֶׁעֲלֵיהֶם אָמַר דָּוִד מַה גָּדְלוּ מַעֲשֶׂיךָ, כַּנּוֹדָע מֵעִנְיַן הַהֶפְרֵשׁ בֵּין מָה רַבּוּ לְמַה גָּדְלוּ שֶׁמָּה רַבּוּ קָאֵי עַל פְּרָטֵי הַנִּבְרָאִים שֶׁבְּדוֹמֵם־צוֹמֵחַ־חַי־מְדַבֵּר, וּמַה גָּדְלוּ קָאֵי עַל הַנִּבְרָאִים הַגְּדוֹלִים כְּמוֹ שֶׁכָּתוּב מִזֶּה בְּדִבּוּר הַמַּתְחִיל מִי יִתֶּנְךָ וּבְהַבֵּיאוּר וְהַהַגָּהוֹת לְשָׁם, וְעַיֵּן בְּלִקּוּטֵי תוֹרָה בְּשִׁיר הַשִּׁירִים בְּדִבּוּר הַמַּתְחִיל יוֹנָתִי בְּחַגְוֵי, בְּעִנְיַן הַמַּלְאָכִים שֶׁהַמַּלְאָךְ בִּשְׁלִישׁ הָעוֹלָם עוֹמֵד כו',

וּכְשֶׁצָּרִיךְ לְהִשְׁתַּלְשֵׁל מִן גַּבְרִיאֵל בְּחִינַת הַתַּרְנְגוֹל הַגַּשְׁמִי בְּהֶכְרֵחַ שֶׁיִּהְיֶה רִבְבוֹת מַדְרֵגוֹת הִשְׁתַּלְשְׁלוּת, וְעַל דֶּרֶךְ זֶה מִכָּל בְּחִינוֹת שֶׁבְּרוּחָנִיּוּת צְרִיכוֹת לִהְיוֹת רִבְבוֹת מַדְרֵגוֹת הִשְׁתַּלְשְׁלוּת עַד שֶׁיִּהְיֶה מְקוֹר מְצִיאַת דָּבָר הַגַּשְׁמִי,

וְהִנֵּה אִם הָיָה הִשְׁתַּלְשְׁלוּת לְבַד לֹא הָיָה יָכוֹל לִהְיוֹת מְצִיאַת דָּבָר הַגַּשְׁמִי כְּלָל כִּי הָיָה הַכֹּל רַק רוּחָנִיּוּת, כִּי אִם הָיָה רִיבּוּי רִבְבוֹת מַדְרֵגוֹת הִשְׁתַּלְשְׁלוּת לֹא הָיָה מִתְהַוֶּה מֵרוּחָנִיּוּת גַּשְׁמִיּוּת כִּי אִם הָיָה הַכֹּל רוּחָנִיּוּת, וּכְדֵי שֶׁיִּהְיֶה

---

75. *Bereishit Rabbah* 68:17; *Yalkut Shimoni*, Daniel 1066:10.

76. Although there are myriad stages of progressive evolvement, they all remain spiritual. The creation of physicality (matter) as *something from nothing* can not come about by way of *ilah* (cause) and *alul* (effect), regardless of the amount of degrees that separate the final product from the initial cause. This is because the final *alul* is inevitably affected by the original *ilah* and is contained within the *ilah*—albeit in an undefined state—even before the *alul* emerges into being. If the *ilah* is a spiritual entity, the final product

istence by way of creation of being from nothingness.[76] As the author of *Ikkarim*[77] states: there is no greater instance of the creation of being from nothingness as the creation of physical matter from the spiritual.[78]

So although every single aspect of the creatures of *B'ya* has a spiritual counterpart in the spiritual realm—such as the root of the rooster, which is the angel Gabriel, and on a loftier level, in *Atzilut*, the five attributes of severity of *imma*[79] [*Binah*]—however, there must first be myriad stages of evolvement and then the creature is produced in the manner of being from nothingness.

THREE HUNDRED/THIRTY/THREE

One can likewise understand the statement in *Pirkei d'Rabbi Eliezer*: "From what was the world created? —from the snow beneath the Throne of Glory." Now, if this snow were physical snow as it appears on the physical plane, we would have to ask about *its* origin—just as we ask about the origin of the world. Rather, what is meant by snow is the concept of *yechidot, asirot, me'ot*:[80] The *gimmel* of the word ***sheleg*** (snow) is three in ones (3), the *lamed* is three in tens (30), and the *shin* is three in hundreds (300).[81]

---

can be nothing more than a less refined form of spirituality. Moreover, the final *alul* is initially contained within the first *ilah,* if only in an extremely indistinct form. Physical matter, by definition, can not be contained within spirituality. Matter must therefore be created *ex nihilo* by G-d alone. This is *yesh m'ayin*—being from nothingness.

In contrast to *ilah* and *alul,* matter does not exist within the realm of the spiritual. Its source is therefore called *ayin*—"nothingness"—relative to the mode of being and perception of the *yesh* (the physical being). The emergence of the *yesh* is therefore called *hitchadshut*—originality or innovativeness, since it does not exist at all prior to its creation (*Sefer HaMaamarim 5700*, pp. 121-3).

In addition, the existence of the *yesh* is always dependent upon the *ayin* to bring it into being, since it has no independent existence (*Sefer HaMaamarim 5701*, pp. 8-9). The *yesh* may be compared to a ray of sunshine. If the sun were to suddenly be extinguished, the ray would cease to exist, for it exists only by virtue of the sun's radiant nature (See *Tanya, Sha'ar HaYichud v'haEmunah,* chap 3).

77. 1:23; 4:3. Rabbi Yosef Albo of Spain (c. 1380 – c. 1444). He was a profound religious philosopher and author of the popular *Sefer Ha'ikkarim* (*The Book of Principles*), which discusses the principles of the Jewish faith in great depth.

78. I.e., the epitome of *yesh me'ayin* is apparent specifically with the creation of physicality from spirit.

מְצִיאוּת הַגַּשְׁמִיּוּת זֶהוּ בְּדֶרֶךְ בְּרִיאָה יֵשׁ מֵאַיִן דַּוְקָא, וּכְמַאֲמַר בַּעַל הָעִיקָּרִים שֶׁהִתְהַוּוּת הַגַּשְׁמִיּוּת מִן הָרוּחָנִיּוּת אֵין לְךָ בְּרִיאָה יֵשׁ מֵאַיִן גָּדוֹל מִזֶּה כו',

וְנִמְצָא כִּי הֲגַם שֶׁלְּכָל דָּבָר וְדָבָר מִפְּרָטֵי הַנִּבְרָאִים דִּבְרִיאָה־יְצִירָה־עֲשִׂיָּה יֵשׁ שׁוֹרֶשׁ וּמָקוֹר לְמַעְלָה בְּרוּחָנִיּוּת כְּמוֹ שׁוֹרֶשׁ הַתַּרְנְגוֹל הוּא גַּבְרִיאֵל וּלְמַעְלָה יוֹתֵר בַּאֲצִילוּת הוּא בְּחִינַת ה' גְּבוּרוֹת דְּאִימָּא, הֲרֵי צְרִיכוֹת לִהְיוֹת תְּחִלָּה רִבְבוֹת מַדְרֵגוֹת הִשְׁתַּלְשְׁלוּת וְאַחַר כַּךְ מִתְהַוֶּה הַדָּבָר בְּדֶרֶךְ בְּרִיאָה יֵשׁ מֵאַיִן.

וּכְמוֹ כֵן יוּבַן בְּעִנְיַן מַאֲמָר שֶׁבְּפִרְקֵי דְּרַבִּי אֱלִיעֶזֶר שֶׁאָמַר אֶרֶץ מֵהֵיכָן נִבְרֵאת מִשֶּׁלֶג שֶׁתַּחַת כִּסֵּא הַכָּבוֹד, וְהִנֵּה אִם הָיָה הַשֶּׁלֶג גַּשְׁמִי כְּמוֹ שֶׁהוּא לְמַטָּה הָיִינוּ צְרִיכִין לִשְׁאוֹל מֵהֵיכָן נִבְרָא הַשֶּׁלֶג, כְּמוֹ שֶׁאָנוּ שׁוֹאֲלִין הָאָרֶץ מֵהֵיכָן נִבְרֵאת, אֶלָּא שֶׁעִנְיַן הַשֶּׁלֶג הוּא בְּחִינַת יְחִידוֹת עֲשִׂירוֹת מֵאוֹת, שֶׁהַגִּימֶ"ל הוּא שְׁלֹשָׁה בִּיחִידוֹת, וְהַלָּמֶ"ד הוּא שְׁלֹשָׁה בַּעֲשִׂירוֹת, וְהַשִּׁי"ן הוּא שְׁלֹשָׁה בְּמֵאוֹת,

---

79. IMMA. In kabbalistic terminology, *imma*, or mother, refers to *binah*, understanding, in its integrated form (i.e., where *binah* contains the elements of the other *sefirot*). *Chochmah* and *binah*, wisdom and understanding, are conceived of as the mother and father that give birth to the emotions.

80. YECHIDOT, ASIROT, ME'OT, ALAFIM, REVAVOT. Lit., Units, Tens, Hundreds, Thousands, Tens of Thousands.

Each letter of the Hebrew alphabet has a numeric value. The first nine letters, from *alef* through *tet*, equal one through nine respectively. These single numbers, or units, are named *yechidot*, singles. The next nine letters, *yud* through *tzadik*, equal ten through ninety respectively, and are named *asirot*, tens. The next four letters, *kuf* through *tav*, equal one hundred through four hundred respectively. These are named *me'ot*, hundreds.

(The intermediary numbers are created by combining together single Hebrew characters of different value. For example, one hundred and twenty-three would be *kuf chaf gimmel* – קכג. Five hundred is represented by *tav kuf* – תק. *Tav reish* equals 600, *tav tav kuf* – תתק equals 900, etc. One thousand is represented by a single letter followed by an apostrophe. For example, 1001 would be written: *alef ' alef* – א'א.)

81. As explained in the previous footnote, the third letter, *gimmel*, equals three. The *lamed* and the *shin* equal 30 and 300 respectively.

So the origin of the world is [*sheleg,* i.e.,] "ones tens and hundreds," which means: *malchut, Z'a,* and *binah.*[82] I.e., there must be myriad stages of evolvement, after which the physical earth is created in a manner of being from nothingness.

And according to the version of the *Midrash* (*Rabbah, Bo,* beg.) that reads "from the *earth* beneath the Throne of Glory,"[83] [the world was created from] *malchut* alone,[84] as known from what is ex-

---

82. In Kabbalistic terms, the concept of *yechidot, asirot, me'ot* (explained in footnote 80) corresponds to the *sefirot.* Rabbi DovBer explains this in his *Biurei Hazohar* (12c):

"Units" refer to *malchut,* "tens" to *z'a,* "hundreds" to *mochin* (intellect, *chochmah* and *binah*), and "thousands" to *keter* (crown), as it is written (Exodus 34:7) *Notzer chesed la'alafim* (He preserves kindness for two *thousand* generations). The word *notzer* has the same letters as *ratzon*—will, which is the character of *keter.* (For the relationship between will and *keter,* see *On the Essence of Chasidus* (Kehot), pp. 8-9.)

To explain: The tremendous amount of gradations causes G-d's Light to be reduced progressively until *malchut* remains only "one" out of a thousand while *z'a* is ten out of a thousand.

An analogy: A teacher cannot possibly transmit an idea on his own level to a student; he can only transmit a small portion since the student is on a far lower intellectual level. Were the student to teach a person less knowledgeable than himself, the idea would once again be reduced and merely a tenth of the student's grasp of the concept would be transmitted to the recipient, and so on.

Similarly, as the concealment of the Divine begins, *keter* receives a tenth of G-d's Light, and in turn, conveys a tenth of that to *mochin. Mochin* then conveys a tenth of that to *z'a,* which in turn conveys a tenth of that to *malchut.*

"In Psalms 68:18 it is written, *rechev elokim ribotayim* (The chariots of G-d are twice ten thousand,) and in Deut. 33:2 it is written, *v'ata merivevot kodesh* ([G-d came from Sinai…] and brought some of His holy myriads), which refers to G-d Himself being "related" to the number ten thousand. Subsequently, *keter*—which receives a tenth—receives one thousand, as in the verse mentioned above. A tenth—or "hundred"—is emanated to *mochin,* of which a tenth emanates to *z'a*—"ten." Finally *malchut*—which receives a tenth of that—is one alone by itself—"single."

The size of the tenth which *malchut* is given does not allow itself to be divided, and hence it remains one. However, the size of the tenth which *z'a* receives allows itself to be divided into ten, and the size of the tenth which *mochin* gets allows itself to be divided into one hundred. The magnitude of the tenth which *keter* receives allows itself to be divided into one thousand. Thus, since *keter* is a tenth, its Emanator (G-d) must "equal" ten thousand because the higher level is ten times the size of the level under it, i.e., a tenth of the higher level contains the entire level below it. Hence the aforementioned verse, *the chariots of G-d are twice ten thousand.*

An analogy in human terms: The head contains all different types of energy for the diverse functions of the body, nevertheless, the head has its own quality,

וְנִמְצָא כִּי מִבְּחִינַת יְחִידוֹת עֲשִׂירוֹת מֵאוֹת הֵם בְּחִינַת מַלְכוּת וְזָ״א [זְעֵיר אַנְפִּין] וּבִינָה הוּא שׁוֹרֶשׁ הָאָרֶץ, וַהֲרֵי צְרִיכוֹת לִהְיוֹת רִבְבוֹת מַדְרֵגוֹת הִשְׁתַּלְשְׁלוּת וְאַחַר כַּךְ מִתְהַוָּה בְּדֶרֶךְ בְּרִיאָה יֵשׁ מֵאַיִן בְּחִינַת מְצִיאַת הָאָרֶץ הַגַּשְׁמִי.

וּלְגִירְסַת הַמִּדְרָשׁ רַבָּה רֵישׁ פַּרְשַׁת בֹּא שֶׁגּוֹרֵס מֵעָפָר

---

since the former fact is only the lowest level of the head's functions.

(This concept applies to the four worlds too. The worlds of *Beriah*, *Yetzirah* and *Asiyah* as they are in *malchut* of *Atzilut*, are collectively only one tenth of *malchut* of *Atzilut*. Hence the rule, "as *malchut* of the higher level descends, it becomes *keter* to the next level.")

83. At first glance, this seems to be a different version of the statement of *Pirkei d'Rabbi Eliezer*. However, the two versions as to what the world was created with (snow or earth) are combined by the commentary named *Pirush Maharzu* on *Bereshit Rabbah* 1:6, to the aforementioned verse from Job 37:6, "He says to the snow: Become earth." There he writes:

"As stated in *Pirkei d'Rabbi Eliezer* ch. 3, 'From what was the world created? —from the snow beneath the Throne of Glory' which G-d took and threw upon the water and it became earth, as it is written, 'He says to the snow: *Become earth!...*' And as described at length in *Shemot Rabbah* 13 (*Bo*, mentioned above in *maamar*): 'G-d took earth from beneath the Throne of Glory, threw it on the water and it became earth. The small pebbles found within the earth became mountains and hills.

"To explain: [At the beginning of Creation,] the entire world was filled with water up until the Throne of Glory as stated in *Midrash Tehillim* 93, 'Rabbi B'rachya said: the water reached up until the Throne of Glory as it is written, 'And the Spirit of G-d hovered over the face of the water." When G-d was about to create the world, he froze the water and it became like hail stones. He then crumbled them into thin pieces, like snow, from which earth and dust was formed...This then is the meaning of the (aforementioned) *Midrash* 'He took earth from beneath the Throne of Glory and threw it on the water,' which refers to the snow that He crumbled into pieces thin like dust. He also placed larger pieces within the snow from which the mountains were formed...Meditate upon this well—how the words of our Sages have a simple connotation as well as the secrets hidden in them, although they are indeed profound..."

Hence, in essence, the terms "snow" and "earth" have an identical connotation.

84. In kabbalistic terms, this version refers to the world's creation from a different perspective. The version in *Pirkei d'Rabbi Eliezer*, that the world was created from the snow, refers to "the myriad stages of evolvement," as previously explained. However, the version in the *Midrash* that the world was created from earth refers only to *Malchut* of *Atzilut* and what is created from it, namely, *Beriah Yetzirah* and *Asiyah* (the finite).

In the words of Rabbi Schneur Zal-

plained elsewhere regarding the earth of the floor of the Tabernacle, [which corresponds to] the earth of the supernal Holy Temple, etc.

LIGHT

Similarly, concerning the creation of light, G-d "wrapped" Himself specifically in a white *tallit*, which is the level of "His garment is like white snow."[85] For through the concealing garment, light can be created through myriad stages of evolvement and then in the manner of being from nothingness.[86]

---

man (*Shaar Hayichud v'haEmunah* ch. 7): "The Name which indicates the attribute of His *malchut* (kingship, royalty), may He be blessed, is the name *Adnut* (L-rdship), for he is the "L-rd of the whole earth." Thus, it is this attribute and this Name which bring into existence and sustain the world so that it should be as it is now, a completely independent and separate entity, and not absolutely nullified."

Similarly, in *Iggeret Hakodesh* ch. 20 he writes: "However, it is known that the principal coming to be of the *yesh* and the totally distinct entity, is through *malchut* of *Atzilut*, which becomes the *atik* of *Beriah* for 'there is no king without a people...' The multitude of creatures, and their division, that were created by the force of the One and absolutely Unique *Ein Sof*, it, too, is from the multitude of letters that issue from *malchut*—"The mouth of the L-rd" and "All their Hosts by the breath of His mouth."...Thus *malchut* is called *alma d'itgalya* (the manifest world), because through it is manifested the power of the light of the *Ein Sof* to create something out of nothing—without recourse to cause and effect. The first nine *sefirot*, however, emanated by a casual evolution, while the light of the *Ein Sof* is vested in *chochmah* only. And that is the meaning of "Their beginning is wedged in their end." For *keter* is the mediator between the Emanator and the emanated, and the lowest level of the *Ein Sof* is contained in it. That is why *keter* is called *keter malchut* (crown of sovereignty); for a crown is but for a king, and, also, the lowest level of the *Ein Sof* is the *malchut* of *Ein Sof*. Consequently, from below upwards, *malchut* of *Atzilut*, too, is called *keter*, and especially since through it is the creation of the souls which are *yesh*, separate entities [in the world of *Beriah*]."

Thus, one can view the creation through all the *sefirot* as myriad stages of evolvement, or one can focus only on *malchut*, and its most instrumental role in the creation of the world.

85. Daniel 7:9. The *maamar* now explains the second *Midrash* quoted above concerning the creation of light, in a similar manner to explaining the first *Midrash* concerning the creation of earth, that there must be a spiritual source for every physical creation, which in the case of light, is G-d's "clothing," or "white *tallit*." The clothing conceals G-dly light and allows for the entity of physical light to be created "through myriad stages of evolvement." This verse from Daniel denotes that G-d has "clothing" which is "white," alluding to "light."

86. The term, "myriad stages of evolve-

מִתַּחַת כִּסֵּא הַכָּבוֹד הַיְינוּ מִבְּחִינַת מַלְכוּת לְבַד כְּנוֹדָע מִמַּה שֶּׁכָּתוּב בְּמָקוֹם אַחֵר מֵעִנְיַן עָפָר שֶׁבְּקַרְקַע הַמִּשְׁכָּן, עַפְרָא דְבֵי מַקְדְּשָׁא דִלְעֵילָּא כו׳.

וּכְמוֹ כֵן הוּא בְּעִנְיַן הִתְהַוּוּת הָאוֹרָה שֶׁהוּא מִמַּה שֶּׁנִּתְעַטֵּף בְּטַלִּית לְבָנָה דַוְקָא הוּא בְּחִינַת לְבוּשֶׁיהּ כִּתְלַג חִיוָּר שֶׁעַל יְדֵי לְבוּשׁ הַמַּעְלִים יוּכַל לִהְיוֹת מְצִיאוּת הִתְהַוּוּת הָאוֹר עַל יְדֵי רִבְבוֹת מַדְרֵגוֹת הִשְׁתַּלְשְׁלוּת וְאַחַר כַּךְ בְּדֶרֶךְ בְּרִיאָה יֵשׁ מֵאַיִן כו׳.

---

ment" is more commonly called "*tzimtzum.*" The word *tzimtzum* has two meanings: (1) contraction, condensation; and (2) concealment, occultation. The doctrine of *tzimtzum* refers to a refraction and concealment of the radiating emanation from G-dliness in a number of stages and in a progressive development of degrees, until finite and physical substances become possible.

Prior to creation there is but G-d alone. G-d as He is in Himself is called *Ein Sof*: Infinite, Without Limit (End). Of G-d as *Ein Sof* nothing can be postulated except that He is *Ein Sof*: "High above all heights and hidden beyond all concealments, no thought can grasp You at all...You have no known Name for You fill all Names and You are the perfection of them all" (*Tikkunei Zohar*, intro. 17a-b).

Rabbi Schneur Zalman writes (*Likkutei Torah Devarim* 46c; *Shir Hashirim* 20d): "The creation of the worlds is not by way of a development from cause to effect...for even myriads upon myriads of occulations and evolutions from grade to grade in a causal process will not avail the development and coming into being of physical matter—not even the matter of the firmaments—out of an evolution from spirit. Rather, it is the power of the blessed *Ein Sof* (Infinite), the Omnipotent, to create...ex nihilo, and this is not by way of a developmental order but by way of a 'leap.'"

Hence, the creation of a non-divine and finite entity requires in the process of emanation a "radical step," a "leap" or "jump" (*dilug*; *kefitzah*) which breaks the gradualism and establishes a radical distinction between cause and effect: a radical act of creation. Only after that has occurred can there be an evolutionary process culminating in finite and material entities.

When it arose in the divine will to create the world, the first act in the creative process was to bring about space in which the divine emanations and ultimately the evolving, finite world could have a place to exist as opposed to becoming dissolved in the divine light. This "primordial space" was brought about by a contraction or "withdrawal" and concentration of divinity into Itself; the omnipresent, infinite Light of the *Ein Sof* was "withdrawn" into Himself; that is, it was screened, dimmed, hidden and concealed, and where it was dimmed—where this occultation and concealment of the light occurred—an "empty" place, a "void" (*makom panuy*; *chalal*) evolved into primordial space. This is *tzimtzum harishon*, the act of the first *tzimtzum*, the radical act of *dilug* and *kefitzah*, as it were: an act of

THE LION

And so it is with all the aspects of the creatures. For example, the root of the lion is the lion of the Chariot.[87] And although [the physical lion] comes about through a "shattering," as known,[88] nevertheless, [the supernal lion] is its source and origin. The evolvement

---

divine self-limitation, so to speak, as opposed to revelation.

In the second phase of the creative process an overt ray or radiation of the divine Light is made to beam into the primeval space of the *chalal*. This thin ray or "line" (*kav*) is the source of the subsequent emanations; it is both the creative and the vivifying force of the creation; it is the immanence of G-d in creation while the concealed light is the all-encompassing transcendence of G-d taking in all creation. However, the *kav* itself also undergoes a series of numerous, successive contractions and concealments, the "myriad stages of evolvement" discussed above.

87. MERKAVAH: Ezekiel (ch. 1) tells of his vision of the Divine Chariot and throne:

"I saw there was a storm-wind coming from the north, a great cloud and a blazing fire, and from its midst like the pure luminescence from the midst of fire. And from its midst [I saw] the image of four *chayot* (angelic creatures)...And the image of the faces was: The face of a man, and the face of a lion on its right...and the face of an ox on the left...and the face of an eagle...And the complexion of the *chayot*—their appearance was like fiery coals...The *chayot* ran and returned as the appearance of a flash of lightning.

"As I observed the *chayot*, I saw one *ofan* (angelic being) on the floor [of the firmament] at the side of each of the *chayot*...The appearance of the *ofanim* and their work was like chrysolite...when the *chayot* moved, the *ofanim* moved beside them, and when the *chayot* raised themselves from the ground, the *ofanim* raised themselves...Above the firmament which is over their heads was the likeness of a throne, in appearance like sapphire, and upon the likeness of the throne was a likeness with the appearance of a man [as it were] upon it above...This was the appearance of the likeness of the glory of the L-rd..."

It is known that every physical creation must have a celestial source, from which it receives its life-force and existence. Its very being and physical characteristics are synonymous to their spiritual source, albeit physical. All living creatures are derived from the spiritual angels that are found in the divine chariot and consequently, the faces of the lion and the ox in the divine chariot are the sources for all physical animals and beasts. Moreover, the *chayot* which have the faces of a lion and an ox are the aspect of *gevurah*, as it is written in Ezekiel 1: 13 "burning like the appearance of torches," and the angels known as *serafim* derive their name from "coals of fire." Thus, physical animals that evolve from these angels are strong and powerful, and their flesh is red, the color of "anger" or "severity" (*Likkutei Torah*, *B'ha'alotcha* 31c-d).

All the beasts derive their energy from the face of the lion, all the animals from the face of the ox and all the birds from the face of the eagle (*Torah Or* 41b).

The two souls of every Jew, the G-dly soul and the animal soul, are also rooted in the chariot. However, the G-dly soul's source is known as "Adam," man, as it is

וּכְמוֹ כֵן יוּבַן בְּכָל פְּרָטֵי הַנִּבְרָאִים כְּמוֹ עַל דֶּרֶךְ מָשָׁל מְצִיאַת הָאַרְיֵה לְמַטָּה שֶׁשָּׁרְשׁוֹ הוּא מִבְּחִינַת הָאַרְיֵה שֶׁבַּמֶּרְכָּבָה, רַק שֶׁזֶּהוּ בְּדֶרֶךְ שְׁבִירָה כו׳ כְּנוֹדָע וְעִם כָּל זֶה הוּא שׁוֹרֶשׁ וּמָקוֹר, וַהֲרֵי בִּכְדֵי שֶׁיִּשְׁתַּלְשֵׁל מִבְּחִינַת הָאַרְיֵה שֶׁבַּמֶּרְכָּבָה

---

written in Genesis (1:27), "And G-d created man in His image," and in Ezekiel 1:26 it is written, "upon the likeness of the throne a likeness with the appearance of a man." In creation of the G-dly soul and its descent to this world, the light found within the *sefirot*—the origin of man—descends to this world, passing through the chariot and specifically its human face, which is thus considered a more proximate source of the G-dly soul.

The animal soul is rooted not in the *sefirot* but in the chariot. It then descends to a lowly derivative (dregs) of the *ofanim*, which are of a lower order than the *chayot*. The animal soul is derived from the "dregs" of the *ofanim*, but is originally rooted in the face of the ox of the divine chariot. (*Likkutei Torah*, *Vayikra* 2b)

In addition to all physical living creatures finding their source in the chariot, the "negative forces" are rooted in the "storm-wind…a great cloud and a blazing fire" amid which Ezekiel beheld his vision. These forces refer to the three totally impure *kelipot*, which contain absolutely no good, and are the source of any thought, speech or action by mankind in transgression of a negative command in the Torah (*Tanya* ch. 1; ch. 6; *Likkutei Torah*, *Chukat* 60a).

88. Rabbi Schneur Zalman explains in *Likkutei Torah*, *Matot* 82c: "The ten *sefirot* are G-dly. How then, were the Worlds of *B'ya*, which are limited creations, created from them? How can *Atzilut* be the energy of *B'ya*—they are two opposites?

The answer is, by way of the *shevirat hakeilim* of *tohu*. For when the vessels of *Tohu* broke and the "shards" thereof fell from the upper realm into lower depths, they became *yesh*. The meaning of *shevirat hakeilim* is "a shattering of the letters." An analogy: A word consists of two or more letters. When the letters are joined together in the proper order they form a word, a "vessel" for a concept. If you break up the word into separate letters, the concept vanishes. An earthenware barrel is subordinate to the wine it contains. When the barrel breaks, the shards are no longer subordinate to the wine.

Similarly, the *sefirot* are conceived under two aspects, namely *or* (light) and *keli* (vessel), standing in relation to each other as form to matter. However, the character of the divine *sefirot* in *Tohu* is described in terms of "abundance of light and paucity of vessels." In other words, the light was too intense to be controlled or contained. This led to *shevirat hakelim*, the "breaking of the vessels," a process whereby the intense divine light was substantially shut off, so to speak, and only "sparks" thereof fell from the upper realm into lower depths. By a further process of infinite reductions and contractions (*tzimtzum*), the divine emanations eventually materialized into Four Worlds." (See also *Mystical Concepts in Chassidism*, ch. 7; *The Unbreakable Soul*, Kehot, p.22, fn. 17.)

Thus, the lofty spiritual aspect of the face of the lion on the divine chariot eventually materialized into the physical lion of our world.

of the lion of the chariot, which proclaims "Holy!"[89] into a physical, predatory lion requires myriad stages of evolvement. And afterwards, in a manner of being from nothingness, the physical lion comes into being.

In truth, the lion is rooted in a far loftier source. For in *Atzilut*, the attribute of *chesed* is also like the lion of the chariot in *B'ya*.[90] As known, the *chayot* (beasts) are in *Yetzirah*; in *Beriah* they are the *cherubim*, i.e., Michael and Gabriel, as stated in the *Zohar*;[91] and in *Atzilut* they are *chesed* and *gevurah*, the supernal chariot.

On an even higher level, *chochmah* is called *aryeh* (lion), since *aryeh* is made up of the letters that form the word *r'eeyah* (sight). [Sight is related to *chochmah*[92]] as it is written, "He *saw* the *beginning* for himself..."[93] alluding to the level of "the *beginning* of *chochmah*."[94]

---

89. Cf. Ezekiel 1:10, Isaiah 6:2-3 and Hosea 11:10. *Likkutei Torah, Bamidbar* pp. 10a ff. combines all three verses and discusses this at length.

90. Elsewhere (*Zot Chukat Hatorah 5629*), Rabbi Shmuel elaborates: Each level of *seder hishtalshelut* is a metaphor for a higher level. For example, a physical lion is only a metaphor for the lion of the Chariot, which proclaims "Holy!" and "Blessed!" The lion of *Beriah* is only a metaphor for *chesed* of *Atzilut*, which is also called "lion." The lion of *Atzilut*, which is the *chesed* of *Atzilut*, is only a metaphor for *chochmah* which is also called lion, as it is written, "He *saw* the *beginning* for himself..." alluding to the level of "the *beginning* of *chochmah*." *Aryeh*, lion, has the same letters as *r'eeyah*, vision. The lion of *chochmah* is only as a metaphor for *keter*, which is also called lion as it is written, "When the lion roars, who does not fear?" It is written in the *Midrash* that this is the speech of "*Anochi*, I am G-d," which is *keter*. See footnote 96 and 98.

The Tzemach Tzedek (*Or Hatorah, Shavuot* p. 221) explains that the celestial lion refers to a revelation of G-d's greatness. Moreover, the term *Anochi* is used rather than *Ani*, although they share the same translation, because the Hebrew letter *chaf* added to the word stands for *keter*, indicating the relationship between *Anochi* and *keter*. The revelation of such a profound level is compared to the roaring of a lion. Just as the lion's roar instills fear into those who hear it, similarly, as the verse continues, when G-d speaks, i.e., reveals Himself, "who does not prophesy," meaning, "who does not experience this tremendous revelation," which at Mount Sinai, when G-d actually declared *Anochi* caused everyone to tremble (see Exodus 19:16; 20:16).

91. This statement is actually found in a commentary to *Zohar* I:18a, *Mikdash Melech*, in the name of the Arizal. Elsewhere (*Seh Tamim 5629*), Rabbi Shmuel cites the above source.

To explain: The angels of the chariot are described as having four faces: man, lion, ox, and eagle. They are known as *chayot*. The angels in each one of the four worlds are of different types, so to

שֶׁאוֹמֵר קָדוֹשׁ בְּחִינַת הָאַרְיֵה שֶׁלְּמַטָּה שֶׁטּוֹרֵף וְדוֹרֵס צְרִיכוֹת לִהְיוֹת תְּחִלָּה רִבְבוֹת מַדְרֵגוֹת הִשְׁתַּלְשְׁלוּת, וְאַחַר כַּךְ בְּדֶרֶךְ בְּרִיאָה יֵשׁ מֵאַיִן מִתְהַוֶּה הָאַרְיֵה הַגַּשְׁמִי,

וּבֶאֱמֶת יֵשׁ שׁוֹרֶשׁ הָאַרְיֵה גַּם הַגְּבֵהַ לְמַעְלָה יוֹתֵר, שֶׁבַּאֲצִילוּת בְּחִינַת הַחֶסֶד הוּא גַּם כֵּן כְּמוֹ בְּחִינַת הָאַרְיֵה בַּמֶּרְכָּבָה דִבְרִיאָה־יְצִירָה־עֲשִׂיָּה, וּכְנוֹדָע שֶׁהַחַיּוֹת הֵם בִּיצִירָה וּבִבְרִיאָה הֵם הַכְּרוּבִים שֶׁהֵם מִיכָאֵל וְגַבְרִיאֵל כְּמוֹ שֶׁכָּתוּב בְּזֹהַר, וּבַאֲצִילוּת הֵם בְּחִינַת חֶסֶד וּגְבוּרָה מֶרְכַּבְתָּא עִילָּאָה,

וְעוֹד גָּבוֹהַּ יוֹתֵר הִנֵּה בְּחִינַת הַחָכְמָה נִקְרֵאת אַרְיֵה שֶׁאַרְיֵה הוּא אוֹתִיּוֹת רְאִיָּה וּכְתִיב וַיַּרְא רֵאשִׁית לוֹ שֶׁהוּא

---

speak. In the world of *Asiyah*, the angels are *ofanim*, which are of a lower order than the *chayot* in the world of *Yetzirah*. In *Beriah* they are *cherubim*; and in *Atzilut* they are *chesed* and *gevurah*—the supernal chariot.

92. Sight emanates from *chochmah*, as in the statement (*Tamid* 32a): "Who is a wise man? One who foresees the result." Foresight is dependent on wisdom, *chochmah*. Thus, the *chachamim* are called "the eyes of the congregation." *Chochmah* is spiritual sight, since the essence of intellect is to grasp a concept and understand it. This is similar to sight, which also consists of grasping and becoming acquainted with an object. Hence, "a fool goes in darkness" (Ecclesiastes 2:14), meaning, one who lacks intellect is as one who walks in darkness and does not see anything. Similarly, one who lacks intellect cannot see spirituality, i.e., wisdom. Physical sight is derived from the outer dimension of intellect, as explained in science that eyesight is derived from the outer dimension of the brain (*Derech Mitzvotecha*, 70a).

93. Deut. 33:21. On the literal level, the verse refers to the tribe of Gad, who chose as their portion the part of the Land of Israel that was conquered first and in which Moses was buried. Kabbalistically, the phrase is seen as an allusion to the relationship between sight and *chochmah*, which is the *beginning* of everything (see next note).

94. The expression "beginning of *chochmah*" is from Psalms 111:10: "The beginning of wisdom is awe of G-d…" Kabbalistically, the phrase alludes to the idea that *chochmah* is the beginning of everything. One of the aspects of *chochmah* is that it is the first of the immanent or indwelling *sefirot*. This is why it is called the beginning. The aforementioned verse from Psalms is translated as "*chochmah* is the first, the head," i.e., the first of the immanent *sefirot*, the beginning and root of all immanent being. While *keter* is the all-encompassing *sefirah, from which* all other *sefirot* are generated, *chochmah* is the first *sefirah* to be generated.

Chochmah is also called the life-force of all of creation. The account of creation be-

Hence, the sages are called, "eyes of the congregation."[95]

On an even higher level, *keter*[96] is also called lion, as it is written, "When the lion roars, who does not fear? When G-d the L-rd speaks, who does not prophesy?"[97] And it is written[98] that this roar refers to the utterance of "I am the L-rd your G-d."[99] This is because 3 *yadot*[100]

---

gins with the word *Bereishit*—"In the beginning." *Targum Yonatan* translates *Bereishit* as *b'chuchmata*—"with *chochmah*," for this *sefirah* is also the instrument of creation. I.e., it permeates all of creation. This is the meaning of the verse, "You made everything with *chochmah*" (Psalms 104:24). In this sense, Scripture refers to *chochmah* as the life-force of all of creation as in the verse, "*chochmah* gives life to all that possess it" (Ecclesiastes 7:12).

Chochmah is called *reishit* for it is the root of the succeeding attributes (Zohar I:3b). *Chochmah* represents the first creative activity of G-d; it is the initial divine instrument of actual creation. The *Ein Sof*, through the mediation of *keter*, is "vested" in *chochmah*, and thereupon creation begins. See *Tanya* I, ch. 35; *Iggeret Hakodesh*, sect. IV, note 25. (See also *Mystical Concepts in Chassidism*, Kehot, p. 71 ff.)

95. Numbers 15:24.

96. KETER: Literally *crown*; *Keter* is the intermediate category between the essence of the Emanator and the emanations. It is thus the source of the ten *sefirot* of the world of *Atzilut*. *Keter* is so lofty that it is referred to in the *Zohar* (III:256b) as *Temira d'kol Temirin*—the most hidden of all. It is for this reason that *keter* is sometimes excluded from the scheme of *sefirot* (*da'at* is counted instead). Since it is their source, it is in a category of its own.

97. Amos 3:8.

98. *Shemot Rabbah* 29:9. See also *Or Hatorah*, *Drushim L'Shavuot* p. 221; *Drushim L'Rosh Hashanah* p. 1428; discourse on this verse, *Nach* p. 447. In *Or Hatorah*, *Yitro* p. 931, *Meorei Or* is quoted that 'lion' is the level of *keter*. However, in this *maamar*, Rabbi Shmuel does not discuss this but proceeds to explain that G-d Himself is the Lion, and His roar was the utterance of "I am the L-rd your G-d."

99. Exodus 20:2.

100. 3 YADOT: In the Torah, there are three expressions of G-d's Hand: *Yad Ha'gdolah*—the Great Hand (Exodus 14:31), *Yad Hachazakah*—the Strong Hand (ibid 6:1), *Yad Ramah*—the High Hand (ibid 14:8).

Rabbi Schneur Zalman elaborates in *Likkutei Torah*, *Nasso* 21b ff.: "These three hands established the *Mishkan* and *Beit Hamikdash*, as it is written, 'The shrine of G-d Your Hands have founded' (Exodus 15:17). The Talmud (*Ketubot* 5a) relates, Bar Kapara taught: 'The deeds of the righteous are greater than the creation of heaven and earth. Regarding creation it is written, 'My hand has founded the earth and My right hand has measured out the heavens' (Isaiah 48:13). This means, one hand was used for each creation (as it is written, 'He turned to his left and created earth; he turned to his right and created the heavens.') However, regarding the deeds of the righteous it is written, 'The place which You O L-rd, have made for Your abode, the Sanctuary which Your

בְּחִינַת רֵאשִׁית חָכְמָה, וְלָכֵן נִקְרָאִים הַחֲכָמִים עֵינֵי הָעֵדָה,

וְעוֹד גָּבוֹהַּ יוֹתֵר הִנֵּה גַּם הַכֶּתֶר נִקְרָא אַרְיֵה כְּמוֹ שֶׁכָּתוּב אַרְיֵה שָׁאָג מִי לֹא יִירָא ה' אֱלֹקִים דִּיבֶּר מִי לֹא יִנָּבֵא וְאִיתָא בִּסְפָרִים שֶׁקָּאֵי עַל דִּבּוּר אָנֹכִי ה' אֱלֹקֶיךָ, שֶׁנִּקְרָא גַּם כֵּן

---

hands, O L-rd, have established.' The word "Hands" is written in plural, even in one deed, the *Beit Hamikdash*.'

"Kabbalistically, the 3 Hands correspond to the 3 categories of *tzimtzum* (fn. 86), *hitpashtut* (diffusion) and *hamshacha* (flow). These are alluded to in the first 3 letters of G-d's Ineffable Name, Y-H-V-H. The *yud*, the smallest letter, refers to *tzimtzum*; the *hey*, a bigger letter, refers to *hispashtut*; while the *vav*, a vertical line, refers to *hamshacha*. These letters "found" the *Beit Hamikdash*—the final *hey*, which alludes to the descent and revelation of G-d's light in this world.

"The relationship of these 3 categories to the 3 hands can be explained as follows: the word *yad* ("hand" in Hebrew) has a numerical value of 14. This equals the four letters of G-d's Name plus the ten letters that are "the filling" of the original four letters.

"To explain: When writing the Hebrew letter א, for example, one can either write the one letter, or one can spell out the syllables of the actual letter as if it were a word, thus: אלף (*Alef*). This practice is common when calculating the numerical value of a given word and one is short of the correct equation. Hence, in calculating the numerical value of י־ה־ו־ה, one begins with 4, since there are four letters, but then when the individual letters are entirely spelled out as they sound, the result is: יוד־הא־ואו־הא, which equals 10 letters. This is now added to the aforementioned 4. Hence, the word *"yad"* had the numerical value of G-d's Name with its filling, (*milui* in Hebrew).

"The "fillings" of the letters of G-d's Name can be done with 3 different letters. One, *milui yuddin* (a filling using *yuds* to spell out each letter—יוד־הי־ויו־הי) has the numerical value of 72. Another, *milui yudin alfin* (a filling using *yuds* and an *alef*—יוד־הי־ואו־הי) equals 63. A third, *milui alfin* (a filling using *alefs*—יוד־הא־ואו־הא) equals 45.

"The Name equaling 72 is in *chochmah* which corresponds to the *yud* (*tzimtzum*), the Name equaling 63 is in *binah* which corresponds to the first *hey* (*hitpashtut*), and the Name equaling 45 is in *z'a* which corresponds to the *vav* (*hamshacha*)."

"The first verse in the Torah, "*Bereshit bara...*" contains 28 letters. This corresponds to the two Hands used in creation (twice *yad* (14) equals 28). These 2 Hands correspond to *chesed* and *gevurah*, as it is written, "L-rd, Yours is the *g'dulah* (greatness) and the *gevurah* (power)." *G'dulah*, or *g'dolah*, is one Hand (*chesed*), while the other is *chazakah* (power, or strength—*gevurah*). The third hand, *ramah*, unites these two opposing attributes for it radiates to them from a source higher than them both" (*Sefer Hamaamarim* 5633 vol. 2 p. 360).

Yad Hagdolah and *Yad Hachazakah* are written with the letter *hey* as a prefix, meaning *the* great or strong Hand, denoting Hands that are "known" to us:

Yad Hagdolah corresponds to man's love of G-d (*chesed*; *ahava*), the love that arouses man to cleave to G-d and is un-

[i.e.] 3 times [G-d's Name of] 72 [letters] equals 216, which is the numerical value of *aryeh*, lion.[101]

So the lion exists even on the highest plane. And each form of the lion comes into being from the one before it through the process of evolvement, followed by the creation of being from nothingness. So it is with every aspect of the worlds of mineral, vegetable, animal and human.

DAY AND NIGHT

Similarly, day and night below and above [are related.] When Moses was on the mountain, how did he recognize day and night? In one instance,[102] our Sages state that when he was taught the Written Torah, he knew it was day. And when he was taught the Oral Torah, he knew it was night. In another instance,[103] our Sages state that when the angels proclaimed "Holy,"[104] he knew it was day. And when they proclaimed "Blessed,"[105] he knew it was night.[106]

---

derstood and felt in the heart. Similarly, fear of G-d (*gevurah*; *yirah*) is alluded to in *Yad Hachazakah*. One feels this in the heart, subjugating oneself by accepting the yoke of Heaven in reciting *Shema*.

In contrast, *Yad Ramah* is written without the *hey* prefix. This is the aspect of *teshuvah*, when man is 'uplifted' higher than ever, a realm in which one has no grasp or comprehension. Hence it remains 'unknown.' (*Torah Or*, 95c-d)

101. Apparently, the Rebbe mentions the concept of the 3 *Yadot* in order to present the idea of multiplying G-d's Name by 3. The connotation of "3 x G-d's Name" is pertinent to the "3 *Yadot*" as follows: Although each *Yad* refers to a different numerical value denoted by specific "fillings" of letters, here the Rebbe takes one of these fillings explained in the previous footnote, 72, and multiplies it by 3. The result is 216, which equals *Aryeh*. The 72-lettered name is the Name of *Gevurah*, severity, the character of the lion.

102. The *Midrashim* (*Shemot Rabbah* 47:8; *Yalkut Shimoni*, *Tissa* 406; *Midrash Tehillim* 19:3; *Tanchuma*, *Tissa* 36) expound: "It is written (Exodus 34:28) '[Moses] remained there with G-d [on Mt. Sinai] for forty days and forty nights.' However, there is no 'night' on High, for it is written (Psalms 139:12), "Even the darkness obscures nothing from You; and the night shines like day—the darkness is as light.' How then, did Moses know how long he spent on Mt. Sinai and how did he know when it was night? For it is written (Deuteronomy 10:10), 'I stood on the mountain.' It is also written (Deuteronomy 9:9), 'I sat on the mountain.' [To reconcile these two seemingly contradictory verses the *Midrash* continues:] When G-d would speak to Moses he knew it was day and when he would tell him 'Review your studies' he knew it was night. Thus, King David states (Psalms 19:3), 'Day to day speech streams forth [and night to night expresses knowledge.']" The commentaries (*Pirush Maharzav*; *Y'dei Moshe*; *Y'fei To'ar*)

אַרְיֵה, וְהַיְינוּ כִּי ג׳ יָדוֹת ג׳ פְּעָמִים ע״ב עוֹלֶה רי״ו כְּמִנְיַן אַרְיֵה כו׳,

וְנִמְצָא כִּי יֵשׁ בְּחִינַת אַרְיֵה עַד רוּם הַמַּעֲלוֹת שֶׁכָּל בְּחִינוֹת אַרְיֵה מִתְהַוֶּה זֶה מִזֶּה בְּדֶרֶךְ הִשְׁתַּלְשְׁלוּת הַמַּדְרֵגוֹת, וּמֵהֶם אַחַר כַּךְ בְּדֶרֶךְ בְּרִיאָה יֵשׁ מֵאַיִן. וְכֵן עַל דֶּרֶךְ זֶה בְּכָל דָּבָר וְדָבָר מְדוֹמֵם־צוֹמֵחַ־חַי־מְדַבֵּר,

אוֹ מִמַּה שֶּׁלְּמַטָּה הוּא יוֹם וָלַיְלָה וּלְמַעְלָה כְּשֶׁהָיָה מֹשֶׁה בָּהָר מֵאַיִן הָיָה יוֹדֵעַ יוֹם וָלַיְלָה הִנֵּה פַּעַם אָמְרוּ רַבּוֹתֵינוּ זִכְרוֹנָם לִבְרָכָה כְּשֶׁהָיוּ לוֹמְדִים עִמּוֹ תּוֹרָה שֶׁבִּכְתָב יָדַע שֶׁהוּא יוֹם וּכְשֶׁלָּמְדוּ עִמּוֹ תּוֹרָה שֶׁבְּעַל פֶּה יָדַע שֶׁהוּא לַיְלָה, וּפַעַם אָמְרוּ רַבּוֹתֵינוּ זִכְרוֹנָם לִבְרָכָה כְּשֶׁהַמַּלְאָכִים אָמְרוּ קָדוֹשׁ יָדַע שֶׁהוּא יוֹם וּכְשֶׁאָמְרוּ בָּרוּךְ יָדַע שֶׁהוּא לַיְלָה,

---

explain: Moses 'stood' out of fear of G-d who was teaching him the Written Torah during the daytime. Then, at night, when G-d would leave Moses to review his studies—the Oral Torah—he would 'sit.' This is the manner of study: during the day the student studies with his teacher, and at night he sits alone to delve profoundly into his studies. For this reason the verse by King David is quoted: *Day to day speech streams forth*—during the day, the teacher conveys his speech and it is the time for the student to pay attention; *and night to night expresses knowledge*—at night the student meditates to comprehend what he was taught by day.

103. *Shemot Rabbah*, *Yalkut Shimoni* and *Midrash Tehillim* ibid.

104. Isaiah 6:3: "Holy, holy, holy is the L-rd of hosts; the whole earth is filled with His glory."

105. Ezekiel 3:12: "Blessed be the glory of the L-rd from its place."

106. To define the connection of *kadosh* to day and *baruch* to night, the Tzemach Tzedek writes (*Or Hatorah* on *Tehillim*, *Yahel Or* p. 62): "See the discourse beginning *'Ka Miflegi'* in *Likkutei Torah*, *Tazria*, [where it is mentioned that] the source of *kadosh* is from *keter* and it is also in *tiferet*, which ascends until *keter*. Thus, we can say that *kadosh* corresponds to 'day' which is in *z'a*. The source of *baruch*, as explained there, is from *chochmah* and *malchut*, similar to 'King Solomon shall be blessed ' (I Kings 2:45). Thus, *baruch* is at 'night,' which is *malchut*."

DAY AND NIGHT: The *Zohar* (II:93a-b) states: "It is written (Genesis 1:4), 'there was evening and there was morning; one day.' There is no night without day and no day without night. They are called "one" only when they are united..." Based on this passage from the *Zohar*, Chasidic texts explain that "day" refers to *z'a*, while "night" refers to *malchut*:

The six days of creation correspond to the six *midot* of *Atzilut*, *z'a*. On the first

Now, there is no comparison at all between physical day and night and [their spiritual counterpart] the Written Torah and the Oral Torah. The Torah is called, "Primordial metaphor,"[107] meaning that Torah is a metaphor with which to understand the *Or Ein Sof*, blessed is He, whose existence preceded the world. And although a metaphor conceals its subject to some extent, nevertheless, the metaphor allows one to understand the subject.

Similarly, "Holy" and "Blessed" are both declarations of selflessness. The *serafs* declare their selflessness with "Holy" because they perceive how G-d is holy and transcendent. Even the ophanim's declaration of "Blessed," which expresses their desire for the drawing forth of [Divine light],[108] is also an expression of selflessness and cannot be compared to physical day and night.

Nevertheless, they are the source for day and night, as is evidenced by the fact that Moses recognized day and night from them. So in the heavenly realms, "day" is the Written Torah, or "Holy," and "night" is the Oral Torah, or "Blessed." And there must be myriad stages of evolvement, followed by the creation of being from nothingness [before a being can come into existence], as

---

day, i.e. with the *midah* of *chesed*, G-d said, "Let there be light"—kindness equals a revelation from one person to another. On the second day, i.e. with the *midah* of *gevurah*, G-d created the firmament—a strong, firm matter. Subsequently, the creations of each day were in accordance with their spiritual counterpart (*Biurei Hazohar*, p. 717).

The essence of *z'a* is that of an emanator, revealing the light of G-d to *malchut*, its recipient. Similarly, during the daytime it is light (*B'Shaah Shehikdimu 5672*, vol. 3 p. 1355).

The night is the attribute of *malchut*, as the verse states, "*Malchutcha malchut kol olamim*" (Your kingship is a kingship over all the worlds). The word *olam* is from the word *he'elem*—concealment or darkness. The light of G-d with which He created the world was hidden and concealed to enable physical creation. Thus, *malchut* is called night which is dark—i.e.—the *tzimtzum* and concealment of *Or Ein Sof* (*Torah Or*, 37a; *Or Hatorah*, *Lech L'cha* p. 73b).

The unity of *z'a* and *malchut* parallels the unity of day and night, resulting in "one day" quoted above from the *Zohar*.

KADOSH AND BARUCH: In the aforementioned *maamar* (*Likkutei Torah*, *Tazria* 22b), it is explained: *Kadosh* is related to *keter*, for *keter* is "holy and separated," i.e. removed, from the *sefirot* and the worlds. However, note that the term used is "*kadosh*," which in Hebrew is spelled with a *vav*, and not "*kodesh*," without a *vav*. The *vav* denotes a flow from *ko-*

הִנֵּה אֵין עֲרוֹךְ כְּלָל בְּחִינַת יוֹם וָלַיְלָה הַגַּשְׁמִי לְגַבֵּי תּוֹרָה שֶׁבִּכְתָב וְתוֹרָה שֶׁבְּעַל פֶּה שֶׁהֵם בְּחִינַת מְשַׁל הַקַּדְמוֹנִי, וְהַיְינוּ שֶׁהַתּוֹרָה הִיא מָשָׁל לְהָבִין בְּחִינַת אוֹר אֵין סוֹף בָּרוּךְ הוּא קַדְמוֹנוֹ שֶׁל עוֹלָם, שֶׁהֲגַם כִּי הַמָּשָׁל מַסְתִּיר קְצָת עַל הַנִּמְשָׁל מִכָּל מָקוֹם עַל יְדֵי הַמָּשָׁל מְבִינִים הַנִּמְשָׁל כו׳,

אוֹ עִנְיַן קָדוֹשׁ וּבָרוּךְ שְׁנֵיהֶם בְּחִינַת הַבִּיטוּל, רַק שֶׁהַבִּיטוּל דִּשְׂרָפִים שֶׁאוֹמְרִים קָדוֹשׁ הוּא מִצַּד שֶׁמַּשִּׂיגִים אֵיךְ שֶׁהוּא יִתְבָּרֵךְ הוּא קָדוֹשׁ וּמוּבְדָּל, וּבָרוּךְ אוֹמְרִים הָאוֹפַנִּים שֶׁרוֹצִים הַהַמְשָׁכָה, וּמִכָּל מָקוֹם הוּא גַּם כֵּן בְּחִינַת הַבִּיטוּל וְאֵינוֹ עֶרֶךְ לִבְחִינַת יוֹם וָלַיְלָה הַגַּשְׁמִיִּים

וּמִכָּל מָקוֹם שֹׁרֶשׁ יוֹם וָלַיְלָה הוּא מֵהֶם שֶׁהֲרֵי מֹשֶׁה יָדַע מִזֶּה, וְנִמְצָא כִּי לְמַעְלָה בְּחִינַת יוֹם הוּא תּוֹרָה שֶׁבִּכְתָב אוֹ קָדוֹשׁ, וּבְחִינַת לַיְלָה הוּא עִנְיַן תּוֹרָה שֶׁבְּעַל פֶּה וּבְחִינַת בָּרוּךְ כו׳, שֶׁצְּרִיכוֹת לִהְיוֹת רִבְבוֹת מַדְרֵגוֹת הִשְׁתַּלְשְׁלוּת תְּחִלָּה,

---

desh—Or Ein Sof, which in itself is beyond any relationship with creation. This is the aspect of *keter*, which would be *kodesh*, holy on its own, even without creation. *Kadosh* however, with the *vav*, denotes a flow from *kodesh ha'elyon*, (the supernal *kodesh*), which is the ray of *keter* that illuminates *z'a*. Now, *z'a* is called *kadosh*, for the *vav* has the image of a downward line, alluding to the flow. Thus, *z'a* and *keter* are related (*Sefer Hamaamarim 5635* vol. 2 p. 221-222.).

Baruch is in *malchut*, for *baruch* means *hamshacha*, flow, as explained in footnote 108. This is related to *malchut* from the verse '*King Solomon shall be blessed*,' meaning, he received the blessing until he became *baruch*, "a blessed one." Moreover, *malchut* is the recipient of the flow from the six *midot* (*Likkutei Torah*, ibid.).

Hence, when Moses heard the angels proclaim *kadosh* he knew it was day, for they are both related to *z'a*, and when they proclaimed *baruch* he knew it was night, for they are both related to *malchut*.

107. Rashi on I Samuel 24:14.

108. *Bracha* has the connotation of *hamshacha* from the term in *Kilayim* 7:1 "*Hamavrich et hagefen*"—one who "kneels" a vine, by bending its top downwards back into the ground and bringing the top back out of the ground. This is done so that the vine can take new root, thus supplying more life-force to the vine from the ground.

explained above. And so it is with literally every aspect of all of creation.

HIDDEN ROOTS

Now, the concept of *creatio ex nihilo* is that the creating force hides from the created being. This is the difference between evolvement and *creatio ex nihilo*. Evolvement means that the evolved state recognizes its source. This means that the evolved state recognizes the lowest element of its source [i.e., its most immediate source], as in the case of intellect and emotions.[109] For this reason *ilah v'alul* is called *histalshelut* [which contains the word *shalshelet*, chain], since a chain consists of a number of rings that are attached to each other.[110]

In *creatio ex nihilo*, on the other hand, the source of the created being is entirely beyond the realm of the created being. That is why the source is called *ayin*, "nothing," since from the perspective of the created being its source is "nothing." If it would be aware of its source, it would not constitute physical existence.

So everything that is physically created from its spiritual source must first evolve through myriad stages of evolvement, in which it enjoys a perception similar to *ilah* and *alul*,[111] and afterwards, the source is concealed from the evolved entity until the entity becomes a created being. This is called "from nothing," meaning that the source is not evident, since it hides.

THE WORLD IS REAL

Accordingly, even if we will say that the existence of the world is real—

indeed, if it is not real, what, then, was created during the six

---

109. Emotions exist within intellect and thus recognize their source. To explain: pondering about a given object gives rise to a desire for it, prior to an actual revelation of a love for it. This is a performance of the emotions while they are still within intellect, before being revealed in the heart. Moreover, even after the emotions emerge in the heart in their entirety, they continue to be nourished by the intellect. For the person desires the object because he had previously pondered it and had come to the conclusion that it was good for him.

Hence, as the *maamar* explains, it is called *hishtalshelut*, for emotions and intellect can be compared to a chain—its strength is the fact that its rings are attached to each other.

The *alul*, (emotion), does have a cer-

וְאַחַר כַּךְ בְּדֶרֶךְ בְּרִיאָה יֵשׁ מֵאַיִן וְכַנַ"ל, וְכֵן הוּא בְּכָל פְּרַט דָּבָר וְדָבָר שֶׁבְּכָל מַעֲשֵׂה בְרֵאשִׁית כו'.

וְהִנֵּה עִנְיַן בְּרִיאָה יֵשׁ מֵאַיִן הוּא שֶׁדָּבָר הַמְהַוֶּה מִסְתַּתֵּר מִבְּחִינַת דָּבָר הַמִּתְהַוֶּה שֶׁזֶּהוּ הַהֶפְרֵשׁ בֵּין הִשְׁתַּלְשְׁלוּת לִבְחִינַת בְּרִיאָה יֵשׁ מֵאַיִן, שֶׁעִנְיַן הַהִשְׁתַּלְשְׁלוּת הוּא שֶׁהֶעָלוּל מַשִּׂיג הָעִילָּה שֶׁלּוֹ וְהַיְינוּ שֶׁבְּחִינָה הַתַּחְתּוֹנָה שֶׁבָּעִילָּה מוּשֶּׂגֶת לִבְחִינַת הֶעָלוּל הַמִּתְהַוֶּה מִמֶּנָּה, כְּמוֹ שֵׂכֶל וּמִדּוֹת, וְלָכֵן נִקְרֵאת הִשְׁתַּלְשְׁלוּת כְּמוֹ הַשַּׁלְשֶׁלֶת שֶׁטַּבַּעַת אַחַת דְּבוּקָה בַּחֲבֶרְתָּהּ כו',

אֲבָל עִנְיַן בְּרִיאַת הַיֵּשׁ מֵאַיִן הִנֵּה בְּחִינַת הָאַיִן אֵינוֹ מוּשָּׂג כְּלָל שֶׁזֶּהוּ פֵּירוּשׁ מֵאַיִן שֶׁאֵינוֹ מוּשָּׂג מִמָּה נִתְהַוָּה בְּחִינָה זוֹ, וְאִם הָיָה מוּשָּׂג לֹא הָיָה מִתְהַוֶּה מְצִיאַת הַגַּשְׁמִיּוּת כו',

וְנִמְצָא כִּי בְּכָל דָּבָר הַנִּבְרָא בְּגַשְׁמִיּוּת מִשָּׁרְשׁוֹ שֶׁבְּרוּחָנִיּוּת תְּחִלָּה מִשְׁתַּלְשֵׁל רִבְבוֹת מַדְרֵגוֹת הִשְׁתַּלְשְׁלוּת שֶׁהוּא כְּעִנְיַן הַשָּׂגַת עִלָּה וְעָלוּל, וְאַחַר כַּךְ מִתְעַלֵּם מִן הַדָּבָר הַמְהַוֶּה עַד שֶׁמִּתְהַוָּה מְצִיאַת יֵשׁ שֶׁל הַנִּבְרָא מֵאַיִן שֶׁאֵינוֹ מוּשָּׂג לְפִי שֶׁמִּתְעַלֵּם כו'.

וְעַל פִּי זֶה יוּבַן שֶׁגַּם אִם נֹאמַר שֶׁמְּצִיאוּת הָעוֹלָם וְכָל מַה שֶּׁנִּבְרָא הוּא מְצִיאוּת,

דְּאִם לֹא כֵן מַהוּ שֶׁנִּבְרָא בְּשֵׁשֶׁת יְמֵי בְרֵאשִׁית, שֶׁאִם

---

tain degree of recognition and understanding of its *ilah,* (intellect). It knows that it receives its energy from the *ilah*, its source, and that without the *ilah* it would be non-existent. For example, a student recognizes that his knowledge comes from his teacher, without whom he would be ignorant. (*Or Hatorah*, *Bereishit* p. 1053b; *Rosh Hashana* p. 1293)

110. So it is in the phenomenon of evolvement, or as it is called here *ilah* and *alul* (cause and effect), each stage of evolvement is "attached" to and in the same realm as the stage immediately before it (even if it is not totally aware of the earlier stages). See fn. 76.

111. "Cause and effect," another term for evolvement.

days of creation? If we will say that the world only appears to us as real, what, then, is the meaning of "In the beginning [G-d] created" if nothing has been created, and it is all an illusion? One must therefore say that the world truly does exist.

Something of a proof to this can be found in the statement of our Sages in the Mishnah (*Sanhedrin*, end of chapter 7):

> Two people are collecting cucumbers [in a magical way]. One collects and is guilty [of the sin of practicing sorcery], and one collects and is not guilty. The one who actually commits the act [through sorcery] is guilty, and the one who only manipulates the eyes is not guilty.

Now if we will say that the world does not truly exist, why is the sorcerer guilty? He is not doing anything with his sorcery, since there are no cucumbers to begin with. It only appears to us that there are cucumbers. [Rather, the world does exist and] therefore, the one who employs optical illusion is not guilty, since in truth he has not done anything. Furthermore, if we were to say that the world does not exist, then the stoning [of the sorcerer] is also nothing. That would mean that there is no reward and punishment, nor Torah and *mitzvot*—and that cannot be.[112]

Rather, the world does exist; but, every aspect of the creations of *B'ya* has its source and origin in the upper realms. First it evolves from its source in the manner of gradation of stages, and then [it is created] in the manner of being from nothingness, meaning that the creating force hides from the created being. Indeed, if the creating force would be revealed to the created being, the created being would become literally nonexistent.

DISAPPEARANCE BY REVELATION

The proof[113] for this is from the angels, who are *sichlim nivdalim*,[114] the great creatures of whom it is said, "How great are Your works, O G-d!" as explained above. Yet, our Sages say, "G-d extended His little

---

112. That the proof for the fact that the world is a true entity comes from Torah and *mitzvot*—true entities—indicates that man's divine service of Torah and *mitzvot* causes the world to exist and become a *true* entity (*Zeh Hayom*, *5744*).

113. *Mofet* in the original, "a sign."

114. "Separate intelligences," or, "abstract

נֹאמַר שֶׁזֶּהוּ רַק מַה שֶּׁנִּדְמֶה לָנוּ אִם כֵּן מַהוּ שֶׁכָּתַב בְּרֵאשִׁית בָּרָא הֲלֹא לֹא נִבְרָא כְּלָל כִּי אִם שֶׁנִּדְמֶה לָנוּ, לָכֵן בְּהֶכְרֵחַ לוֹמַר שֶׁנִּמְצָא הָעוֹלָם לְיֵשׁ וְדָבָר,

וְכִדְמוּת רְאָיָה לָזֶה מִמַּאֲמַר רַבּוֹתֵינוּ זִכְרוֹנָם לִבְרָכָה בְּמִשְׁנָה סוֹף פֶּרֶק ז׳ דְּסַנְהֶדְרִין

שְׁנַיִם לוֹקְטִים קִשּׁוּאִין אֶחָד לוֹקֵט חַיָּיב וְאֶחָד לוֹקֵט פָּטוּר הָעוֹשֶׂה מַעֲשֶׂה חַיָּיב הָאוֹחֵז אֶת הָעֵינַיִם פָּטוּר,

וְאִם נֹאמַר שֶׁלֹּא יֵשׁ מְצִיאוּת הָעוֹלָם כְּלָל מִפְּנֵי מָה הָעוֹשֶׂה מַעֲשֶׂה חַיָּיב הֲלֹא אֵינוֹ עוֹשֶׂה בְּהַכִּישׁוּף שֶׁלּוֹ כְּלָל מֵאַחַר שֶׁלֹּא יֵשׁ קִשּׁוּאִין כְּלָל כִּי אִם נִדְמֶה לָנוּ שֶׁזֶּה קִשּׁוּאִין כו׳, אֲשֶׁר מִטַּעַם זֶה הָאוֹחֵז אֶת הָעֵינַיִם מֵאַחַר שֶׁבֶּאֱמֶת אֵינוֹ עוֹשֶׂה הֲרֵי הוּא פָּטוּר כו׳, וְאִם נֹאמַר שֶׁאִם לֹא יֵשׁ מְצִיאַת הָעוֹלָם כְּלָל הֲרֵי גַּם הַסְּקִילָה אֵינָהּ כְּלָל, נִמְצָא שֶׁלֹּא יֵשׁ שָׂכָר וְעוֹנֶשׁ וְלֹא יֵשׁ תּוֹרָה וּמִצְוֹת שֶׁזֶּה אִי אֶפְשָׁר כְּלָל,

אֶלָּא הָעִנְיָן הוּא דְּבֶאֱמֶת מְצִיאַת הָעוֹלָם הוּא מְצִיאוּת, רַק שֶׁלְּכָל דָּבָר וְדָבָר מִפְּרָטֵי הַנִּבְרָאִים דִּבְרִיאָה־יְצִירָה־עֲשִׂיָּה יֵשׁ שׁוֹרֶשׁ וּמָקוֹר לְמַעְלָה, וּתְחִלָּה מִשְׁתַּלְשֵׁל מִן מְקוֹרוֹ בְּדֶרֶךְ הִשְׁתַּלְשְׁלוּת הַמַּדְרֵגוֹת, וְאַחַר כַּךְ בְּדֶרֶךְ בְּרִיאָה יֵשׁ מֵאַיִן הַיְינוּ שֶׁבְּחִינַת הַמְהַוֶּה מִסְתַּתֵּר מִן הַדָּבָר הַמִּתְהַוֶּה, אֲבָל אִם הָיָה מִתְגַּלֶּה דְּבַר הַמְהַוֶּה עַל הַדָּבָר הַמִּתְהַוֶּה הָיָה נַעֲשֶׂה מִן הַדָּבָר הַנִּתְהַוֶּה אַיִן וְאֶפֶס מַמָּשׁ,

וְהַמּוֹפֵת לָזֶה שֶׁהֲרֵי גַּם הַמַּלְאָכִים שֶׁהֵם שְׂכָלִים נִבְדָּלִים וְהֵם הַנִּבְרָאִים הַגְּדוֹלִים שֶׁעֲלֵיהֶם נֶאֱמַר מַה גָּדְלוּ מַעֲשֶׂיךָ וְכַנַּ״ל הִנֵּה

---

intelligences." This is a common term in philosophical works referring to the supernal creatures or creations, devoid of any material content. They are pure spirit and, therefore, distinguishable (or separated) from one another only by their differing degrees of intellectual apprehension. (Cf. *Moreh Nevuchim* 1:49; *Ikkarim* 2:12.)

finger among them and consumed them."[115] This means that when more than their allotted portion [of Divine light necessary for their existence] is revealed to them they are entirely nullified. And if such a revelation would come upon other creatures, they would certainly become entirely nonexistent.

It follows, then, that even when they are not confronted with such revelation and they exist as independent beings, they are not truly existent.

TRANSIENCE = NONEXISTENCE

The proof for this is from the rivers that dry up once in seven years and [therefore] cannot be used to sanctify the waters of the red heifer.[116] Even though the waters are now flowing normally, they are invalid—even as they flow—because their flow is interrupted once in seven years.[117]

Now, our Sages have said, "For six millennia the world will exist and for one millennium it will lie fallow."[118] Like the river, once in

---

115. CONSUMED ANGELS. When G-d sought to create man, He created a group of ministering angels and asked them: "Is it your will that we create man in our image?" They replied: "Master of the Universe, what are his deeds?" G-d said: "Such and such will be his deeds [both good and evil (*Maharsha*)]." They said: "Master of the Universe! *What is man that You should remember him, the son of man that You should be mindful of him* (Psalms 8:5)?" G-d then extended His little finger among them and consumed them (*Sanhedrin* 38b).

The extending of G-d's "little finger" refers to a revelation of the tenth and lowest of the ten *sefirot, malchut,* the source for creation. When this source is revealed to the created entity, the entity loses its being (*Likkutei Torah, Rosh Hashanah* 60b; see also *Siddur im Dach* 152a). By consuming the angels through revelation, G-d answered their question regarding the value of the creation of man: Man, through the fulfillment of G-d's will on the physical plane, would transcend the limitations inherent to creation and *would* be able to receive revelation without losing his existence. See *Likkutei Sichot* vol. 10, p. 52, fn. 28 and *Sefer Hamaamarim 5663* p. 9 ff.

116. THE RED HEIFER. The Torah (Numbers 19:1-21) prescribes the manner in which a person that has come in contact with a corpse can be purified. This involves the slaughtering and burning of a perfectly red heifer, whose ashes are then mixed with what the Torah calls "living waters." This mixture is then sprinkled upon the impure person.

The law cited here from the Mishnah (*Parah* 8:9) qualifies what the Torah means by "living waters," saying that this excludes, among other things, rivers that dry up once in seven years (or less).

117. The question arises: why are rivers

אָמְרוּ רַבּוֹתֵינוּ זִכְרוֹנָם לִבְרָכָה הוֹשִׁיט הַקָּדוֹשׁ בָּרוּךְ הוּא אֶצְבָּעוֹ הַקְּטַנָּה בֵּינֵיהֶם וּשְׂרָפָם, פֵּירוּשׁ שֶׁכַּאֲשֶׁר נִתְגַּלָּה עֲלֵיהֶם יוֹתֵר מֵהַחוֹק הַקָּצוּב לָהֶם נִתְבַּטְּלוּ לְגַמְרֵי, וְכָל שֶׁכֵּן כְּשֶׁהָיָה מִתְגַּלֶּה עַל שְׁאָרֵי הַנִּבְרָאִים הָיָה נַעֲשֶׂה מֵהֶם אַיִן וְאֶפֶס לְגַמְרֵי,

וְאִם כֵּן גַּם בְּעֵת אֲשֶׁר אֵינוֹ מִתְגַּלֶּה עֲלֵיהֶם וַהֲרֵי הֵם נִמְצָאִים לְיֵשׁ וְדָבָר מִכָּל מָקוֹם אֵינָם מְצִיאוּת אֲמִיתִּי,

וְהָרְאָיָה לָזֶה מִנְּהָרוֹת הַמְכַזְּבִים שֶׁמְּכַזְּבִין אַחַת בַּשָּׁבוּעַ הַיְינוּ אַחַת לְשֶׁבַע שָׁנִים הֲרֵי הֵם פְּסוּלִים לְקִידּוּשׁ מֵי חַטָּאת, וַהֲגַם שֶׁכָּעֵת הֵם הוֹלְכִים בְּטוֹב רַק מֵאַחַר שֶׁאַחַת לְשֶׁבַע שָׁנִים נִפְסָק הִילוּכָן הֵם פְּסוּלִים גַּם בְּעֵת שֶׁהוֹלְכִים,

וְאִם כֵּן הֲלֹא אָמְרוּ רַבּוֹתֵינוּ זִכְרוֹנָם לִבְרָכָה שִׁית אַלְפֵי שְׁנֵי הָוֵי עָלְמָא וְחַד חָרוּב שֶׁנִּמְצָא אַחַת בַּשָּׁבוּעַ הֵם מְכַזְּבִים

---

that dry up every *eight* years or more considered to be living waters? Does not their eventual cessation indicate that they too are transient and that even as they flow they are not truly "alive"?

The answer is that since the entire world is transient—it is destroyed in the seventh millennium, as mentioned below—one must say that what the Torah means with "living waters" is waters that are "alive" within the context of the properties of nature. And since every seven-year cycle is considered to be a complete period (see the classic commentators on the beginning of *parshat Behar*, Leviticus 25, in explanation of why the seventh year is a year of emancipation), any river that flows for at least that amount of time is considered to be alive within the context of the natural world. See *Likkutei Sichot* vol. 6, p. 92.

118. *Sanhedrim* 97a. Due to the profound revelation of *Or Ein Sof*, the physicality of the world—as it is now, in a state of *yesh*—will be unable to receive energy from there. This is referred to as "it will be destroyed," i.e., nullified and in a state of nothingness. Subsequently, a new world will be constructed, which will not interfere with the revelation of *Or Ein Sof*, as it is written (Isaiah 66:22), "the new heavens and the new earth which I will create." (*Likkutei Torah*, *Bamidbar* 4c)

This does not mean that the world will be destroyed. Rather, just as the existence of the world is divine will and it remains as strong and fresh as the beginning of creation, likewise its decay is divine will. The meaning of "for one millennium it will be destroyed" is that the world will not be physical, but this is not to imply that G-d's Energy will cease. The universe, heaven and earth, will be elevated to a lofty realm and will not be of coarse matter, but not that it will decay. (*B'Shaah Shehikdimu 5672*, vol. 2 p. 685)

Throughout the course of the six mil-

seven years[119] the world "dries up" and ceases to exist. So even when the world does exist, it is not a truly existent being. Furthermore, if the Creator wills it, the creating force of the world can be revealed to the created being and it will all become nonexistent.

This coincides with Rambam's comment on the verse, "The L-rd, G-d is true," meaning that "He alone is true and no other being possesses truth like His truth....This is what the Torah means with the words, 'There is nothing else besides Him,' meaning that there is no true being besides Him that is like Him....."

This will also explain why Yonathan translates ["Who is like You among the supernal beings" as] "There is none like You among the supernal beings."[120] This means that even the supernal beings are creations, being from nothingness; and by the will of the Creator, their source can be revealed to them, thereby nullifying their existence completely. This indeed occurred when "G-d extended [his small finger among the angels and consumed them.]" So even now [when they *do* exist], their existence is not a true one, and thus "there is none like You," since, "He alone is true and no other being possesses truth like His truth."

THE FOUR ELEMENTS

According to Onkelos' translation—"There is nothing besides You"—we can say the following[121]: When you carefully examine the nature of all physical beings, when you contemplate them well, you will find that all "physical" beings are not [truly] physical. Take the substance of wood, for example, which is made up of the four elements: fire, air, water, and earth. Although it contains each of the four elements, its substance is not any one of them. Rather, its primary being is the power that combines the four elements. It follows,

---

lennia, the Jewish nation has had ups and downs, peaceful times and disturbed times. Each descent was for the purpose of a subsequent higher ascent. However, the seventh millennium is the climax of all ascents; there is none higher. It is the apex of all exalted realms and elevations, and thus, it is called *menucha*, rest, over which nothing transcends (*Torah Or*, 96a).

119. "Years" meaning "millennia" in this context.

120. *Yonathan* actually translates "Who is like you among the supernal beings," as quoted at the beginning of the *maamar*. However, "who is like you..." conveys the

וְנִפְסָקִים, לָכֵן גַּם בָּעֵת אֲשֶׁר הָעוֹלָם נִמְצָא הוּא גַּם כֵּן אֵינוֹ מְצִיאוּת אֲמִיתִי, וּמַה גַּם אֲשֶׁר בִּרְצוֹת הַבּוֹרֵא יוּכַל לְהִתְגַּלּוֹת דָּבָר הַמְהַוֶּה עַל הַדָּבָר הַמִּתְהַוֶּה וְיִהְיֶה אַיִן וָאֶפֶס מֵהַכֹּל כו׳.

וְזֶהוּ שֶׁכָּתַב הָרַמְבַּ״ם עַל פָּסוּק וַה׳ אֱלֹקִים אֱמֶת, הוּא לְבַדּוֹ הָאֱמֶת וְאֵין לְאַחֵר אֱמֶת כַּאֲמִיתָּתוֹ כו׳ וְזֶהוּ אֵין עוֹד מִלְּבַדּוֹ, שֶׁאֵין שָׁם אֱמֶת מָצוּי מִלְּבַדּוֹ כְּמוֹתוֹ כו׳.

וְעַל פִּי זֶה יוּבַן מַה שֶּׁתִּרְגֵּם יוֹנָתָן לֵית כְּוָותָךְ בְּאֵילֵי מְרוֹמָא שֶׁגַּם אֵילֵי מְרוֹמָא הֵם נִבְרָאִים יֵשׁ מֵאַיִן וּבִרְצוֹת הַבּוֹרֵא יָכוֹל לְהִגָּלוֹת עֲלֵיהֶם שָׁרְשָׁם וּמְקוֹרָם וְיִתְבַּטְּלוּ לְגַמְרֵי וּכְעִנְיַן הוֹשִׁיט כו׳ לָכֵן גַּם עַכְשָׁיו אֵינָם קִיּוּם אֲמִיתִּי וְלָכֵן לֵית כְּוָותָךְ כִּי הוּא לְבַדּוֹ הָאֱמֶת וְאֵין לְאַחֵר אֱמֶת כַּאֲמִיתָּתוֹ.

וּלְפֵירוּשׁ הַתַּרְגּוּם אוּנְקְלוֹס שֶׁפֵּירֵשׁ לֵית בַּר מִינָּךְ יֵשׁ לוֹמַר דְּהִנֵּה כַּד דַּיְיקַת שַׁפִּיר בְּכָל דְּבָרִים הַגַּשְׁמִיִּים כְּשֶׁתִּתְבּוֹנֵן בָּהֶם הֵיטֵב תִּמְצָא שֶׁגַּם כָּל דְּבָרִים הַגַּשְׁמִיִּים הֵם אֵינָם גַּשְׁמִיִּים, וְהוּא עַל דֶּרֶךְ מָשָׁל מְצִיאַת הָעֵץ הִנֵּה הוּא מוּרְכָּב מִד׳ יְסוֹדוֹת אֵשׁ רוּחַ מַיִם עָפָר, וְעִם כָּל זֶה הֲגַם כִּי יֵשׁ בּוֹ כָּל הַד׳ יְסוֹדוֹת מִכָּל מָקוֹם מְצִיאוּתוֹ אֵינוֹ אֶחָד מִן הַיְסוֹדוֹת הַנַּ״ל כִּי אִם עִיקָּרוֹ הוּא כֹּחַ הַמַּרְכִּיב אֶת הַד׳

same meaning as "there is none like you."

121. In the *maamar Usfartem Lachem 5736* (*Sefer Hamaamarim 5736* p. 215), the Rebbe, of blessed memory, explains that according to Yonathan, physical reality is compared to an axe in the hand of the woodchopper which has no identity of its own and is entirely controlled by the woodchopper. In other words, physical reality does exist but it is not comparable to the existence of G-d: Who is like You? Onkelos, however, is expressing the idea that there is indeed *nothing* besides You, not even a subjugated existence. It is not clear whether this is the intention in this maamar as well.

then, that its primary substance is the thing that [combines the elements and thereby] creates and sustains it, namely, the utterance [of G-d.[122]]

When the wood is burned, all that remains is ash, which is from the element of earth within the wood. The three elements—fire, water, and air—leave through the smoke. Nevertheless, the ash itself also contains the four elements. So the true essence of even ash is not any one of the four elements, but rather the thing that creates it and sustains it. And when all of the elements separate, nothing remains. It is clear, then, that the true essence of all physical beings is the power that combines [the four elements], which is the [divine] utterance that gives it life and creates it every moment. And when all of the elements separate, nothing remains.

CONCEALMENT AND LIMITATION

Hence, it is clear that there is no physical substance that is independent of G-dliness. For in reality, the power of concealment [of Divinity] is as Divine as the power of revelation. Hence the verse: "I will wait for *Havayah*[123] [G-d], even though He hides His face...."[124]

---

122. THE UTTERANCE OF G-D. In Avot 5:1 we read: "The world was created by means of ten (divine) utterances." Chasidut explains that the ten utterances are actually the life-force which sustains the entire universe, as stated in *Tanya,* ch. 20: "In the case of the Holy One, blessed be he, His speech is not, heaven forfend, separated from His blessed Self, for there is nothing outside of Him, and there is no place devoid of Him. Therefore, His blessed speech is not like our speech, G-d forbid...His blessed speech is called "speech" only by way of an anthropomorphic illustration, in the sense that, as in the case of man below, whose speech reveals to his audience what was hidden and concealed in his thoughts, so, too, it is with the blessed *Ein Sof,* Whose emitted light and life-force—as it emerges from Him, from concealment into revelation, to create worlds and to sustain them—is called "speech." These emanations are indeed, the ten utterances by which the world was created."

Other creations, not enumerated in the ten utterances, are created from G-d's speech "by means of numerous and various contractions until the created beings can receive their life and existence from it" (*Tanya*, ibid).

In *Shaar HaYichud v'HaEmunah* (ch. 1) Rabbi Schneur Zalman expounds on this subject: "It is written (Psalms 119:89): "Forever, O G-d, Your word stands in the heavens." The Baal Shem Tov, of blessed memory, has explained that "Your Word" which you uttered, "Let there be a firmament in the midst of the waters..." these very words and letters [i.e., the divine creating forces which bring everything into existence *ex nihilo*] stand firmly forever within the firmament of heaven and

יְסוֹדוֹת, וְנִמְצָא כִּי עִיקַּר מְצִיאוּתוֹ הוּא הַדָּבָר הַמְהַוֶּה אוֹתוֹ וּמְקַיְּימוֹ הוּא הַמַּאֲמָר,

וּכְשֶׁשּׂוֹרְפִים הָעֵץ וְנִשְׁאָר רַק הָאֵפֶר שֶׁהוּא יְסוֹד הֶעָפָר הַנִּמְצָא בְּהָעֵץ, וְהַג׳ יְסוֹדוֹת אֵשׁ מַיִם רוּחַ יוֹצְאִין בֶּעָשָׁן, הִנֵּה בְּהָאֵפֶר יֵשׁ גַּם כֵּן ד׳ יְסוֹדוֹת, אֲשֶׁר הָאֵפֶר הוּא גַם כֵּן אֵינוֹ אֶחָד מִן הַד׳ יְסוֹדוֹת כִּי אִם דָּבָר הַמְהַוֶּה אוֹתוֹ וּמְקַיְּימוֹ, וּכְשֶׁתַּפְרִיד כָּל הַיְסוֹדוֹת אָז לֹא יִשָּׁאֵר מְאוּמָה, וְנִמְצָא כִּי כָל דְּבָרִים הַגַּשְׁמִיִּים כְּשֶׁיֶּשְׁנָם אֵיזֶה מְצִיאוּת הִנֵּה עִיקַּר מְצִיאוּתָם הוּא כֹּחַ הַמַּרְכִּיב שֶׁשָּׁרְשׁוֹ מִן הַמַּאֲמָר הַמְחַיֶּה אוֹתוֹ וּמְהַוֶּה אוֹתוֹ בְּכָל עֵת וּבְכָל רֶגַע, וּכְשֶׁתַּפְרִיד כָּל הַיְסוֹדוֹת לֹא יִשָּׁאֵר מְאוּמָה.

וְנִמְצָא כִּי אֵין שׁוּם מְצִיאוּת גַּשְׁמִי זוּלַת אֱלֹקוּת, כִּי בֶּאֱמֶת כֹּחַ הַמַּסְתִּיר הוּא גַם כֵּן אֱלֹקוּת כְּמוֹ כֹּחַ הַנִּגְלֶה, וּכְמוֹ שֶׁכָּתוּב

---

are forever clothed within all the heavens to give them life, as it is written, "The word of our G-d shall stand firm forever"...for if the letters were to depart [even] for an instant, G-d forbid, and return to their source, all the heavens would become naught and absolute nothingness, and it would be as though they had never existed at all, exactly as before the Utterance, 'Let there be a firmament.' And so it is with all created things...if the letters of the Ten Utterances by which the earth was created during the Six Days of Creation were to depart from it [but] for an instant, G-d forbid, it would revert to naught and absolute nothingness, exactly as before the Six Days of Creation."

123. HAVAYAH. The Ineffable Divine Name, or Tetragrammaton, composed of the four letters Y-H-V-H, and pronounced in conversation as *Havayah*. There are many names for G-d in Scripture, each of which expresses a different aspect or attribute of Divinity. *Havayah* refers to G-d the Infinite, transcending creation and nature, time and space completely—the level of divinity which brings everything into existence *ex nihilo*. The name *Elokim* represents the level of G-d which conceals the Infinite Light and life-force, for this Infinite force is too intense for finite creatures to endure. *Elokim* is the power of G-d that makes the world appear as though it exists naturally and independently. Therefore, *Elokim* has the numerical value of the word *hateva* (nature). In the Era of Moshiach, however, the level of *Havayah* will be revealed and perceived throughout nature.

124. Isaiah 8:17.

This means that just as there is the revealed *Havayah* so is there the concealed *Havayah*. The divine powers of concealment and limitation are as divine as the divine power of infinity. As stated in *Avodat Hakodesh*[125]: if you consider G-d to be capable of infiniteness but incapable of limitation, you have detracted from His completeness.[126]

In fact, the source for limitation is loftier than the source for infiniteness, as explained elsewhere regarding the *reshimah* ("impression").[127] See elsewhere regarding [the difference between the levels referred to as] impression, engraving, carving, and action.[128]

---

125. The author of this work, Rabbi Meir ibn Gabbai of Spain and Egypt (16th century), was one of the first and foremost systematists of the Kabbalah. He authored *Derech Emunah*, *Tola'at Ya'akov*, and *Avodat Hakodesh*, which is an elaborate introduction to the Kabbalah, dealing with its most important problems and containing profound critical discussions of various philosophical expositions. It should be noted, though, that Ibn Gabbai's works are pre-Lurianic (*Avodat Hakodesh* was completed in 1531, and *Derech Emunah* in 1539).

126. Part 1 chapter 8.

127. In *Or Hatorah* (*Bereishit* vol. 7, p. 2386) the Tzemach Tzedek explains: When the *tzimtzum* occurred, G-d's infinite light was removed and concealed. However, a *reshimah*, an impression of the light, remained. Subsequently, the *kav*, a thin thread of light, was made to shine through the remaining impression, by way of which the universe was created. This impression is the source of the creation of *keilim* (vessels). Although the *kav* is the aspect of "luminary" and "light," while the *reshimah*, which is latent and is merely the idea of "letters" or "vessels," nevertheless, it is a *reshimah* of the "general light" which illuminated everywhere before the initial *tzimtzum*, and is not just the contracted light of the *kav*.

Hence, although the advantage of the *kav* is apparent because it is "light" and a "revelation," in truth, the *reshimah* is superior, since it is a remaining impression of the *General Light* that preceded the *tzimtzum*. And as mentioned above, the *reshimah* is the source of the *keilim*, i.e., limitations. Thus, it follows that the source for limitation is loftier than the source for infiniteness.

128. RESHIMAH, CHAKIKAH, CHATZIVAH, ASIYAH. In *Maamarei Admur Hazaken* (*Inyanim* p. 388), Rabbi Schneur Zalman identifies these four levels as: 1) *arich* (the lower part of *keter*), 2) *chochmah* and *binah*, 3) *ze'er anpin* and 4) *malchut*.

The highest level in the creation of the world, *reshimah*, is a level where there is merely an "impression" of the *otiyot* (letters used for creation), which are hardly noticeable because they are so subtle. In the descent, this is followed by *chakikah*, an "engraving," which can already be detected. The letters can actually be

וְחִכִּיתִי לַהוי׳ הַמַּסְתִּיר פָּנָיו שֶׁכְּמוֹ שֶׁיֵּשׁ שֵׁם הוי׳ הַנִּרְאֶה כְּמוֹ כֵּן שֵׁם הוי׳ מַסְתִּיר פָּנָיו, שֶׁכֹּחַ הֶהֶסְתֵּר וְכֹחַ הַמַּגְבִּיל הֵם אֱלֹקוּת כְּמוֹ כֹּחַ הַבִּלְתִּי בַּעַל גְּבוּל, וּכְמוֹ שֶׁכָּתוּב בַּעֲבוֹדַת הַקֹּדֶשׁ שֶׁאִם תֹּאמַר שֶׁאֱלֹקוּת הוּא כֹּחַ בִּלְתִּי בַּעַל גְּבוּל וְאֵין לוֹ כֹּחַ בִּגְבוּל אַתָּה מְחַסֵּר שְׁלֵימוּתוֹ,

וּבֶאֱמֶת שֹׁרֶשׁ הַגְּבוּל הוּא נַעֲלֶה יוֹתֵר מִכֹּחַ הַבִּלְתִּי בַּעַל גְּבוּל כְּמוֹ שֶׁכָּתוּב בְּמָקוֹם אַחֵר מֵעִנְיַן הָרְשִׁימָה, וְעַיֵּן בְּמָקוֹם אַחֵר בְּעִנְיַן רְשִׁימָה חֲקִיקָה חֲצִיבָה עֲשִׂיָּה.

"grasped"—similar to engraved letters that are grasped in the stone upon which they are engraved.

Pardes (*shaar* 16, ch. 9) defines *reshimah*: "between the end of *ayin* and the beginning of *yesh*...the subtlest level of *yesh*; there is no difference between *reshimah* and *ayin* (nothingness). Thus, *reshimah* is found in *chochmah*, which is the beginning of *seder hishtalshelut*."

Reshimah is the intermediary between infiniteness and limitation, and is in *Atzilut*. It lies between the *ayin*, nothingness, and the *yesh*. *Atzilut* is the start of the *source* of limitation, while *Beriah* is the start of actual limitation. The *orot* (lights) of *Atzilut* are essentially pure and simple—signifying infiniteness, whereas the *keilim* (vessels) of *Atzilut* signify the power of limitation. Hence, *Atzilut* is the intermediary between the *Ein Sof* and creation (*Maamarim 5666*, p. 509-510).

To understand how the source for limitation transcends the source for infiniteness—see previous footnote.

In human terms, the four aforementioned levels refer to four means of expressing oneself. *Reshimah*, which is merely an impression, is as subtle as *ohr* (light), and corresponds to *chochmah*, the undefined state of potential. For this reason *chochmah* is compared to a flash of lightning, since it constantly flashes in and out of existence. Moreover, *reshimah* is similar to the seminal thought of *chochmah*, "the short manner" in which a teacher should transmit knowledge to a student as it is written (*Pesachim* 3b), "One should always teach his student in a short manner," or the "shorthand" of a scribe or architect, who writes notes that contain far more information than what is written.

Chakikah, signifying actual engraved letters and hence more physical, refers to *binah*, the second step in the thinking process, which actualizes and externalizes what was originated in *chochmah*, developing it to a substantial idea of intellect.

Chatzivah (carving) corresponds to the voice, the next stage in expressing the idea developed in *binah*. Apparently, carving is lower, i.e. more physical than engraving since it refers to carving a design or picture containing more detail than plain letters.

Asiyah, (action) the final stage, refers to speech, truly conveying the ideas of one's intellect (*Sefer Hamaamarim 5710*, p. 73).

This is the meaning of the verse, "Indeed You are a G-d who conceals Himself"[129]: "You" refers to G-d's revealed state, where one can address Him in the second person. And [the verse declares that] just as the revealed state is "You," so it is truly You in the state of concealment, referring to the divine power of concealment.

INHERENT SELFLESSNESS

According to the above, it follows that there is not a thing besides Him. For all physical beings that were created are literally G-dliness, i.e., the word of G-d that creates and sustains them. As stated in *The Book of Beinonim,* (part 2, chapter 3):

> If the eye would be granted permission to see and grasp the life-force and spirit of each creature—that which flows within it from "what proceeds from the mouth of G-d"[130] and 'His breath'—the physicality of the creature, as well as its materiality and tangibility, would not be visible at all to our eyes.
>
> For it is inherently null in relation to its life-force and spirit, since without the spirit it would be naught and absolute nothingness, exactly as before the six days of creation.
>
> And it is only the spirit that flows upon it from what proceeds from the mouth of G-d and His breath that constantly brings it forth from nothingness into being and creates it. Hence, there is truly nothing besides Him.

The meaning of his words, "it is inherently null," is as follows: It is known that "inherent selflessness"[131] is synonymous with what is said about Moses "and we are 'what.'"[132] This is the level of selflessness, where one is free of any vestige of self-awareness. This is also the concept of "without 'what'" mentioned in *Sefer Yetzirah.*[133]

---

129. Isaiah 45:15.

130. Deut. 8:3.

131. As opposed to "imposed selflessness," referred to as *bittul hayesh* ("nullification of being").

132. Exodus 16:7. In the wilderness, when the Jews complained to Moses and Aaron for food, Moses and Aaron began to grow tired of the Jews' constant complaining. They told the Jews: G-d has heard your complaints, which you are actually addressing against Him. What are we? Your complaints are not against us, but against G-d. (I.e., Why do you consider us important enough that you throw all your complaints upon us?)

Chasidut interprets this verse as an ex-

וְזֶהוּ מַה שֶּׁכָּתוּב אָכֵן אַתָּה אֵל מִסְתַּתֵּר, פֵּירוּשׁ אַתָּה הוּא בִּבְחִינַת גִּילּוּי לְנוֹכֵחַ, וּכְשֵׁם שֶׁאַתָּה הוּא בִּבְחִינַת הַגִּילּוּי כְּמוֹ כֵן אַתָּה מַמָּשׁ הוּא מִסְתַּתֵּר הַיְינוּ בְּחִינַת כֹּחַ הַהֶסְתֵּר כו׳.

וְנִמְצָא שֶׁלְּפִי זֶה לֹא יֵשׁ כְּלָל שׁוּם דָּבָר זוּלָתוֹ יִתְבָּרֵךְ, כִּי כָּל הַדְּבָרִים הַגַּשְׁמִיִּים אֲשֶׁר נִתְהַוּוּ הֵם הֵם אֱלֹקוּת מַמָּשׁ בְּחִינַת דְּבַר ה׳ הַמְהַוֵּהוּ וּמְקַיְּימוֹ, וּכְמוֹ שֶׁכָּתוּב בְּסֵפֶר שֶׁל בֵּינוֹנִים חֵלֶק ב׳ פֶּרֶק ג׳

אִלְמָלֵא נִיתְּנָה רְשׁוּת לָעַיִן לִרְאוֹת וּלְהַשִּׂיג אֶת הַחַיּוּת וְהָרוּחָנִיּוּת שֶׁבְּכָל נִבְרָא הַשּׁוֹפֵעַ בּוֹ מִמּוֹצָא פִּי ה׳ וְרוּחַ פִּיו לֹא הָיָה גַּשְׁמִיּוּת הַנִּבְרָא וְחוּמְרוֹ וּמַמָּשׁוֹ נִרְאֶה כְּלָל לְעֵינֵינוּ

כִּי הוּא בָּטֵל בִּמְצִיאוּת מַמָּשׁ לְגַבֵּי הַחַיּוּת וְהָרוּחָנִיּוּת שֶׁבּוֹ מֵאַחַר שֶׁמִּבַּלְעֲדֵי הָרוּחָנִיּוּת הוּא אַיִן וְאֶפֶס מַמָּשׁ כְּמוֹ קוֹדֶם שֵׁשֶׁת יְמֵי בְרֵאשִׁית מַמָּשׁ,

וְהָרוּחָנִיּוּת הַשּׁוֹפֵעַ עָלָיו מִמּוֹצָא פִּי הוי׳ וְרוּחַ פִּיו הוּא לְבַדּוֹ הַמּוֹצִיאוֹ תָּמִיד מֵאַיִן לְיֵשׁ וּמְהַוֶּה אוֹתוֹ אִם כֵּן אֶפֶס בִּלְעָדוֹ בֶּאֱמֶת.

וּבֵיאוּר דְּבָרָיו שֶׁאָמַר שֶׁהוּא בָּטֵל בִּמְצִיאוּת מַמָּשׁ הִנֵּה נוֹדָע כִּי בִּיטּוּל בִּמְצִיאוּת הוּא כְּעִנְיָן מַה שֶּׁכָּתוּב בְּמֹשֶׁה וְנַחְנוּ מָה שֶׁהוּא בִּיטּוּל בְּלִי שׁוּם מְצִיאוּת מַהוּת, וּכְעִנְיַן בְּלִי מָה שֶׁנִּזְכָּר בְּסֵפֶר יְצִירָה,

---

pression of Moses' inherent selflessness, as it is written (Numbers 12:3), "Moses was very humble, more so than any man on the face of the earth."

133. 1:1-3. *Sefer Yetzirah* is one of the oldest written sources of Kabbalah, and is attributed to the Patriarch Abraham. It has been the subject of numerous commentaries since it was first published in Mantua, 1562. "Without 'what'" in Hebrew is '*b'li mah*,' which literally means *b'li mahut*, 'without self-awareness.' Before the ten *sefirot* are actualized into *sefirot*, they exist within the Essence of *Or Ein Sof*. Regarding this stage *Sefer Yetzirah* describes the ten *sefirot* as "without 'what,'" i.e., without any self-awareness or substance.

For the truth is that even the fact that the created being *appears* to be an independent entity [does not constitute separateness from G-d, since] when one contemplates the matter well it becomes apparent that this phenomenon *too* stems from a G-dly force.[134]

The above demonstrates that there is no reality at all outside of G-d. He gives life to and creates all emanations, creations, formations, and physical entities.[135] And He is their existence, their being, and their life. There is no reality at all outside of Him, etc.

ECHAD VS. YACHID

According to the above, we can understand the concept of the commandment to proclaim His Oneness, alluded to in the word *echad* [one].[136] [The meaning of the word *echad* is as follows:] The creation of the seven heavens, one earth[137] and the four corners of the universe,[138] does not constitute a reality outside of Him, since they are entirely nullified, as explained.

This is alluded to specifically in the word *echad*. For the use of the word *yachid* would have implied that G-d is one and indivisible; but [it would have allowed for the notion] that the creations of the six days of creation are an independent reality. The word *echad*, however, alludes to the fact that although a world was created with seven heavens, an earth, and four corners, they are all utterly nullified to the *Alef* [of the word *echad*], the *Aluf* [Master] of the world, Who sustains and creates it all.

About this *echad* it is said that "there is one, there is no other."[139] This means that although *echad* could be used in the context of "one of many," when the word is used in reference to G-d it means "one, and no other." So the meaning of *echad* in this context is identical to *yachid*.

However, the word *echad* is used to allude to the idea that the creation of the seven heavens, the earth, and the four corners [does

---

134. So by using the words "inherently null," Rabbi Schneur Zalman is alluding to the fact that there is nothing at all about the created being that could be considered separate from G-dliness, since even its façade of being is also generated by a G-dly force.

135. These four descriptions allude to the creatures of the four worlds. See above fn. 52 and 62.

וְהַיְינוּ מִפְּנֵי כִּי בֶּאֱמֶת גַּם מַה שֶׁנִּרְאֶה הַנִּבְרָא לִמְצִיאוּת דָּבָר מָה כְּשֶׁתַּשְׂכִּיל הֵיטֵב תִּמְצָא שֶׁגַּם זֶה כֹּחַ אֱלֹקַהּ כו׳,

וְנִמְצָא כִּי לֹא יֵשׁ שׁוּם מְצִיאוּת זוּלָתוֹ יִתְבָּרֵךְ הַמְחַיֶּה וּמְהַוֶּה כָּל הַנֶּאֱצָלִים וְהַנִּבְרָאִים וְהַנּוֹצָרִים וְהַנַּעֲשִׂים וְהוּא הוּא מְצִיאוּתָם וְקִיּוּמָם וְחַיּוּתָם וְאֵין שׁוּם מְצִיאוּת זוּלָתוֹ יִתְבָּרֵךְ כו׳.

וְעַל פִּי כָל הַנַּ״ל יוּבַן עִנְיַן מִצְוַת לְיַיחֲדוֹ שֶׁמְּרוּמָּז בְּתֵיבַת אֶחָד, הַיְינוּ שֶׁהֲגַם שֶׁנִּבְרְאוּ ז׳ רְקִיעִים וָאָרֶץ וְד׳ רוּחוֹת הָעוֹלָם מִכָּל מָקוֹם מֵאַחַר שֶׁהֵם בְּטֵלִים לְגַמְרֵי וְכַנַּ״ל, נִמְצָא שֶׁאֵין שׁוּם מְצִיאוּת זוּלָתוֹ יִתְבָּרֵךְ,

וְזֶהוּ מְרוּמָּז בְּתֵיבַת אֶחָד דַּוְקָא, שֶׁאִם הָיָה נֶאֱמָר יָחִיד הָיָה נִשְׁמָע שֶׁאֱלֹקוּת הוּא יָחִיד וּמְיוּחָד, אֲבָל הַנִּבְרָא בְּשֵׁשֶׁת יְמֵי בְרֵאשִׁית הוּא מְצִיאוּת, אֲבָל כְּשֶׁנֶּאֱמַר אֶחָד מְרוּמָּז שֶׁהֲגַם שֶׁנִּבְרָא הָעוֹלָם בְּז׳ רְקִיעִים וָאָרֶץ וְד׳ רוּחוֹת הֵם בְּטֵלִים בְּתַכְלִית לִבְחִינַת הָאָלֶ״ף אַלּוּפוֹ שֶׁל עוֹלָם הַמְחַיֶּה וּמְהַוֶּה הַכֹּל כו׳,

וְעַל אֶחָד זֶה נֶאֱמַר יֵשׁ אֶחָד וְאֵין שֵׁנִי פֵּירוּשׁ הֲגַם כִּי אֶחָד יֵשׁ גַּם אֶחָד הַמָּנוּי אֲבָל אֱלֹקוּת הוּא אֶחָד שֶׁאֵין שֵׁנִי, וְאִם כֵּן פֵּירוּשׁ אֶחָד זֶה הוּא כְּמוֹ יָחִיד,

רַק נֶאֱמַר אֶחָד בִּכְדֵי שֶׁיּוּבַן וִירוּמַּז בְּהַתֵּיבָה שֶׁהֲגַם שֶׁנִּבְרְאוּ ז׳ רְקִיעִים וָאָרֶץ וְד׳ רוּחוֹת מִכָּל מָקוֹם הֵם בְּטֵלִים בְּתַכְלִית לִבְחִינַת הָאָלֶ״ף הוּא אַלּוּפוֹ שֶׁל עוֹלָם הַמְחַיֶּה

---

136. The last word of the verse, "Hear O Israel…."

137. Alluded to in the *chet*, which equals 8, of *echad*.

138. Alluded to in the *dalet*, which equals 4.

139. *Adon Olam, Siddur Tehillat Hashem* p. 13.

not constitute a reality outside of G-d, since] they are entirely nullified to the *Alef*, the Master of the world, Who gives life to and creates all the creations. Thus it is clear that the notion of *sheetuf* is not at all conceivable, since there is no reality outside of Him—so what can we consider a partner to Him?

NEGATING "PARTNERSHIP"

This explains Onkelos' translation of ["Who is like You among the supernal beings"]: "There is nothing besides You." Onkelos here means to negate the notion of *sheetuf*. In other words, although the supernal beings are the greatest creatures, nevertheless, even they are not truly existent. For, at the will of the Creator, more than their allotted portion of [divine energy] can be revealed to them, which would cause them to become entirely nonexistent. This indeed occurred when G-d extended His small finger among [the angels] and consumed them, meaning that they became entirely nonexistent. Similarly, if the Creator wills it, He can reveal [Himself] to the other angels and they will lose their existence.

Therefore, even when they are not confronted with a revelation that exceeds their allotted share, they are not truly existent. Rather, they are messengers through whom sustenance is channeled. They are like the axe in the hand of the woodchopper, which has no freedom of choice at all. It is therefore inconceivable to call them partners [to G-d].

By contrast, G-d granted honor to a father and mother, as in the verse, "Honor your father and mother." This is because there are three partners in the creation of man [G-d, father, and mother]. And the parents are called partners—although their contribution cannot compare to the contribution of G-d—because they at least have freedom of choice. The angels, on the other hand, do not have freedom of choice at all. Rather, they are like an axe in the hand of a woodchopper.

([There are instances where the Sages seem to imply that angels *do* have freedom of choice.] Our Sages relate, "Matat was ejected."[140]

---

140. Matat, also called Matatron, is the king of all the angels (*Zohar* III:282b). He is G-d's servant, the first creature created by G-d, and rules all His heavenly legions (*Midrash Hane'elam* in *Zohar* I:126). In Chasidut, Matat is more commonly re-

וּמְהַוֶּה כָּל הַנִּבְרָאִים כו׳, וְנִמְצָא לְפִי זֶה לֹא שַׁיָּךְ עִנְיַן הַשִּׁיתּוּף כְּלָל מֵאַחַר שֶׁלֹּא יֵשׁ שׁוּם מְצִיאוּת זוּלָתוֹ יִתְבָּרֵךְ וּמַה נְּשַׁתֵּף לוֹ.

וְזֶהוּ שֶׁתִּרְגֵּם אוּנְקְלוֹס לֵית בַּר מִינָּךְ שֶׁהַכַּוָּונָה לְהוֹצִיא עִנְיַן הַשִּׁיתּוּף, וְהַיְינוּ שֶׁהֲגַם שֶׁהַמַּלְאָכִים הֵם נִבְרָאִים הַגְּדוֹלִים מִכָּל מָקוֹם גַּם הֵם אֵינָם מְצִיאוּת כְּלָל, כִּי בִּרְצוֹת הַבּוֹרֵא יִתְגַּלֶּה עֲלֵיהֶם יֶתֶר מֵחוֹק הַקָּצוּב לָהֶם וְיִתְבַּטְּלוּ לְגַמְרֵי וּכְמוֹ שֶׁהָיָה כְּשֶׁהוֹשִׁיט הַקָּדוֹשׁ בָּרוּךְ הוּא אֶצְבָּעוֹ הַקְּטַנָּה בֵּינֵיהֶם שֶׁנִּשְׂרְפוּ פֵּירוּשׁ שֶׁנִּתְבַּטְּלוּ לְגַמְרֵי כְּמוֹ כֵן בִּרְצוֹת הַבּוֹרֵא יוּכַל לְגַלּוֹת גַּם עַל שְׁאָרֵי הַמַּלְאָכִים וְיִתְבַּטְּלוּ מִמְּצִיאוּתָם,

וְלָכֵן גַּם בְּעֵת אֲשֶׁר אֵינוֹ מִתְגַּלֶּה עֲלֵיהֶם יֶתֶר מִכְּפִי חוֹק הַקָּצוּב מִכָּל מָקוֹם אֵינָם מְצִיאוּת אֲמִיתִּית, רַק הֵם שְׁלוּחִים שֶׁעַל יָדָם נִמְשָׁךְ הַהַשְׁפָּעָה וְהֵם כְּגַרְזֶן בְּיַד הַחוֹצֵב בּוֹ בִּלְתִּי שׁוּם בְּחִירָה כְּלָל, וְלָכֵן אֵינוֹ שַׁיָּךְ לִקְרוֹתָם בְּשֵׁם שׁוּתָּף כְּלָל,

כְּמוֹ לְאָב וָאֵם שֶׁחָלַק הַקָּדוֹשׁ בָּרוּךְ הוּא כָּבוֹד כְּמוֹ שֶׁכָּתוּב כַּבֵּד אֶת אָבִיךָ וְאֶת אִמֶּךָ לִהְיוֹת כִּי ג׳ שׁוּתָּפִים בָּאָדָם, נִקְרְאוּ שׁוּתָּפִים הֲגַם כִּי חֵלֶק אָב וָאֵם אֵינוֹ בְּעֵרֶךְ כְּלָל לְחֵלֶק הַקָּדוֹשׁ בָּרוּךְ הוּא מִכָּל מָקוֹם נִקְרְאוּ שׁוּתָּפִים לִהְיוֹתָם בַּעֲלֵי בְחִירָה עַל כָּל פָּנִים, אֲבָל הַמַּלְאָכִים אֵינָם בַּעֲלֵי בְחִירָה כְּלָל, רַק כְּגַרְזֶן בְּיַד הַחוֹצֵב בּוֹ

(וּמַה שֶּׁאָמְרוּ רַבּוֹתֵינוּ זִכְרוֹנָם לִבְרָכָה אַפְקוּהוּ לְמֶטַ״ט וְכֵן אָמְרוּ רַבּוֹתֵינוּ זִכְרוֹנָם לִבְרָכָה בְּבָבָא מְצִיעָא דַּף פ״ה עַל

---

ferred to as one who fashions crowns for G-d from the prayers of Israel (*Torah Or* 42b from *Zohar* 37b. It must be noted, though, that this *Zohar* relates how the crowns for G-d are fashioned by Enoch. This complies with footnote 142 below.)

Also, in *Bava Metzia* (85b) our Sages state: "They brought Elijah and administered to him 60 lashes of fire" because he had deviated [from the divine plan] and revealed supernal secrets in the lower worlds.[141] However, it can be said that these angels were originally souls. [Elijah was originally human and] Matat was originally Enoch.[142] So it can be said that even now they possess freedom of choice. But other angels do not have freedom of choice and are no more than an axe in the hand of the woodchopper.)

This is the meaning of "Who is like You among the supernal beings, O G-d!"—even among the supernal beings, namely the angels, who are *sichlim nivdalim*,[143] there is nothing besides You. For the truth is that even the body of an angel is made up of two elements, fire and air. As it is written, "He makes the winds His angels, His ministers flaming fire."[144] And the main thing is the sustaining and combining of the elements, which is achieved by the utterance and breath of the mouth of G-d, Who sustains them.

Thus there is nothing besides Him, etc. And consequently, it is impossible to suggest the notion of *sheetuf*, which is to combine the Name of G-d with something else, since the truth is that when one looks closely [one sees that] there is no reality at all outside of him, etc.

See also the footnote on *Sefer Hamaamarim 5708* p. 202.

The Talmud (*Chagigah* 14b-15a) relates how there were four scholars who entered "the garden" (Heaven) by reciting G-d's ineffable Name. They were, Ben Azai, Ben Zoma, Acher and Rabbi Akiva. In reporting what happened to each of these scholars as a result of this experience, the Talmud relates: "Acher looked and "destroyed the plants" (i.e. apostatized. The expression of plants is used in accordance with this incident's opening phrase, which refers to Heaven as "the garden.") What caused him to apostatize? He saw the angel Matat who had permission to sit while recording the merits of Israel. Acher asked, "Hasn't it been taught that in Heaven there is no sitting…and no weariness?" perhaps [G-d forbid] there are two divinities in Heaven? Matat was then ejected and administered sixty blows of fire."

Tosafot *ad loc* adds: This was to show that Matat has no superior power to other angels. Other commentaries explain that Matat should have risen in honor of Acher, and the fiery blows were actually a punishment for his choosing to sit.

141. The Talmud relates the following: Elijah the prophet once revealed to Rabbi Judah the Prince that if Rabbi Chiya and his sons would pray simultaneously, the Messiah would arrive. Rabbi Judah then called a public fast day and during the

אֵלִיָּהוּ וּמַחְיוּהוּ שִׁיתִּין פּוּלְסִין דְּנוּרָא, וְהַיְינוּ מִפְּנֵי כִּי שִׁינָּה וְגִילָּה בָּעוֹלָם הַזֶּה מֵהָרָזִין עִילָּאִין, יֵשׁ לוֹמַר שֶׁהַמַּלְאָכִים אֵלּוּ הָיוּ תְּחִלָּה נְשָׁמוֹת, שֶׁמְּטַ"ט הוּא חֲנוֹךְ, וְאִם כֵּן יֵשׁ לוֹמַר שֶׁגַּם עַתָּה הֵם בַּעֲלֵי בְחִירָה, אֲבָל שְׁאָרֵי הַמַּלְאָכִים הֵם בִּלְתִּי בְחִירָה וְרַק כַּגַּרְזֶן בְּיַד הַחוֹצֵב בּוֹ).

וְזֶהוּ מִי כָמוֹכָה בָּאֵלִים הוי' שֶׁגַּם בְּאֵילֵי מְרוֹמָא הֵם הַמַּלְאָכִים שִׂכְלִים נִבְדָּלִים לֵית בַּר מִינָּךְ, שֶׁבֶּאֱמֶת גַּם גּוּף הַמַּלְאָךְ הוּא מִשְּׁנֵי יְסוֹדוֹת אֵשׁ וְרוּחַ כְּמוֹ שֶׁכָּתוּב עוֹשֶׂה מַלְאָכָיו רוּחוֹת מְשָׁרְתָיו אֵשׁ לוֹהֵט וְהָעִיקָּר הוּא קִיּוּם וְהַרְכָּבַת הַיְסוֹדוֹת שֶׁזֶּהוּ מֵהַמַּאֲמָר וְרוּחַ פִּיו שֶׁל הַקָּדוֹשׁ בָּרוּךְ הוּא הַמְקַיְּימָם,

וְנִמְצָא כִּי לֵית בַּר מִינָּךְ כוּ', וּמִמֵּילָא אִי אֶפְשָׁר לוֹמַר עִנְיַן הַשִּׁיתּוּף שֶׁהוּא לְשַׁתֵּף שֵׁם שָׁמַיִם וְדָבָר אַחֵר שֶׁבֶּאֱמֶת כַּד דַּיְיקִית שַׁפִּיר לֹא יֵשׁ שׁוּם מְצִיאוּת כְּלָל כוּ' זוּלָתוֹ יִתְבָּרֵךְ כוּ'.

---

prayer service ordered Rabbi Chiya and his sons to lead the service. (On a fast day, three people lead the services.) When they reached the prayer of "He restores life to the dead," an allusion to the Messianic era, the world shook. It was said in heaven: "Who revealed secrets in the world?" And the reply was: "Elijah." Elijah was then summoned and administered sixty lashes of fire." This story seems to imply that Elijah, an angel, has freedom of choice and can incur punishment by choosing wrongly.

142. See Yonathan on Genesis 5:24, the verse which discusses Enoch: "Enoch served truthfully before G-d, and he was no more among the inhabitants of the earth because he ascended to heaven by the Word of G-d, Who named him Mitatron the Great Scribe." See also *Yalkut Shimoni*, *Isaiah* sect. 452 that in the World to Come during the process of G-d's re-establishing of the world, G-d "will bring down Enoch, son of Yered whose name is Matatron, and the four *chayot* (angels) from under the wheels of the chariot..."

143. See footnote 114.

144. Psalms 104:4. On the literal level, this verse means that winds and fires are messengers of G-d. In this context, however, the verse is read as a description of the makeup of the bodies of angels.

HEBREW NOTES

HEBREW NOTES

מי כמוכה: **ב"היום יום" כ"ח תמוז, מובא שכ"ק אדמו"ר מהר"ש הי' חוזר על מאמר זה פעמים רבות כדי לטהר את האויר [והובא עד"ז גם בסה"מ תרנ"ט ע' רכג. סה"מ מלוקט ח"א ע' צב. ח"ב ע' קכג].**

ולהלן יצויינו המקומות בספרי אדמו"ר מהר"ש [שנדפסו עד עתה] שבהם נמצא תוכן המאמר:

סה"מ תרכ"ו: 1) מי כמוכה מש"פ בשלח. 2) זכור גו' עמלק — ע' יד. 3) אנכי ה"א — ע' נ. 4) ואהבת — ע' קסב.

סה"מ תרכ"ז: 5) מהיכן זכו ישראל לק"ש — ע' שס (בהוצאת תש"ס — ע' שפו).

סה"מ תרכ"ח: 6) ויקחו לי תרומה — ע' קב. 7) והר סיני — ע' קמז-ח. 8) שמע ישראל — ע' קצ.

סה"מ תרכ"ט: 9) מי כמוכה — פ' יתרו. 10) מי כמוכה — פ' שמיני.

המשך והחרים תרל"א: 11) ס"ע כה-כח.

סה"מ תרל"ד: 12) אני ישנה (פרקים ט-י) — ע' קע ואילך. 13) מים רבים — ע' שעג

המשך מים רבים תרל"ו: 14) פקנ"ה-ק"ס — ע' קע.

לכללות המאמר ראה אוה"ת משפטים (כרך ח) ע' ג'לו ואילך.

ונמצא בשינויים ובאריכות: סה"מ תרמ"ג ע' צה-צט [ד"ה האמנם ישב אלקים]. ד"ה ברוך שעשה ניסים תרס"ד (סה"מ תרס"ד (הוצאת תשנ"ד) ע' קלו). המשך תער"ב ח"ב ע' א'קמא-א'קמד [ד"ה זה היום]. עטר"ת ע' עדר ואילך [ד"ה כי תשא]. תער"ב-ע"ו ע' מו. תרפ"א ע' קג ואילך [ד"ה ראו עתה פט"ו-ט"ז]. תרפ"ו ע' נז ואילך [ד"ה ביום השמע"צ]. תרצ"ז ע' רכא ואילך [ד"ה ואיש כי ימרט]. ה'תשי"א ע' 8 ואילך וע' 34 ואילך [ד"ה תקעו ספ"ב ואילך וד"ה יחיינו מיומיים פי"א]. ד"ה אנכי ה"א — ליל ב' דחה"פ תשכ"ו. ד"ה וספרתם לכם — ב' אייר תשל"ו.

אך הענין יובן . . אין עוד מלבדו: **בהבא להלן בפיסקא זו ושלאחריי: ראה אוה"ת נח (כרך ג) תרנח, א ואילך. שם (כרך ז) תתשסד, ב ואילך. דרמ"צ מצות אחדות הוי' (נט, ב ואילך). וראה גם שם מצות מילה פ"ג (ו, א-ב). אוה"ת יתרו ע' תשנה. ואתחנן ע' שעג.**

שבני נח אין מוזהרי' על השיתוף: **בסה"מ מלוקט ח"א ע' נג מציין: עייג"כ נו"ב מהד"ת חיו"ד סקמ"ח. פ"ת ליו"ד סקמ"ז סק"ב. פרמ"ג בשפתי דעת סו"ס סה. שדי חמד פאת השדה כללים אות ג' ס"ו סקי"א ובספרים שהובאו שם.**

ענין השיתוף אינו ע"ז כלל: **ראה בכ"ז ד"ה את הוי' האמרת תרל"ב (סה"מ ח"ב ע' תעו ואילך). סה"מ תרע"ח ע' תיב ואילך. תרפ"ו ע' קנא ואילך. סה"מ מלוקט ח"א ס"ע ל ואילך וס"ע נב ואילך. וראה גם סה"מ מלוקט ח"ג ע' ק ובהערה 20 שם.**

שארז״ל . . בענין המלאכים: **הובא ונת׳ בסה״מ תרכ״ז (הוצאת תש״ס) ע׳ צז ואילך. תרכ״ח ע׳ קמו ואילך. וראה גם ד״ה אר״ז פתילות ושמנים תרכ״ט.**

ג׳ שותפין באדם אב ואם כו׳ והקב״ה: **נת׳ בארוכה באוה״ת יתרו ע׳ תתקמ ואילך.**

השיתוף הוא ממצות לייחדו . . ה׳ אחד: **ראה דרמ״צ ואוה״ת נח שם.**

מ״ש . . ה׳ אחד . . יחיד: **בהבא להלן [עד סוף הפיסקא]: ראה תו״א וארא נה, ב ואילך. לקו״ת תזריע כג, ג. בלק ע, א. אמרי בינה שער הק״ש פ״ח. שרש מצות התפלה פי״ח (קכד, א־ב). סה״מ תרכ״ו (הוצאת תשמ״ט) ע׳ קצג־ד. תרכ״ז (הוצאת תש״ס) ע׳ רכג ואילך. ובכ״מ. וראה גם ד״ה ענין הגשת יהודה ליוסף וד״ה אר״י יהא חלקי תרכ״ט.**

בת״א בד״ה וארא: **תו״א שם נה, ב ואילך. וראה גם אוה״ת שה״ש (כרך א) ס״ע קלב ואילך. ואתחנן ס״ע תכט ואילך.**

וביאור הענין לקרב אל השכל: **בהבא להלן (עד פיסקא: והנה ענין בריאה יש מאין) ראה בארוכה אוה״ת משפטים (כרך ח) ע׳ ג׳לו ואילך. ד״ה ברוך שעשה ניסים תרס״ד. סה״מ תרכ״ח ע׳ ב־ג.**

וכמ״ש הרס״ג . . שנברא דבר מלא דבר: **בס׳ האמונות והדעות מ״א:** דבר לא מדבר. **וכ״ה במו״נ ח״ב רפי״ג. ואולי גם כאן צ״ל כן. — הערת כ״ק אדמו״ר שליט״א (בהמשך מים רבים תרל״ו שם).**

האורה מהיכן נבראת: **ראה גם סה״מ תש״ד ע׳ 26. ס׳ הערכים־חב״ד כרך ב ע׳ תריז. וש״נ.**

אך הענין הוא שלכל דבר . . יש שורש ומקור ברוחניות: **בהבא להלן ראה גם ד״ה ויצוום בסה״מ תרכ״ז (הוצאת תש״ס) ע׳ צח ואילך. וד״ה והר סיני (והי׳ מספר) בסה״מ תרכ״ח ע׳ קמז ואילך. אוה״ת וארא ס״ע ריז ואילך. ד״ה זאת חוקת תרכ״ט.**

יוצר משרתים . . ואשר משרתיו . . כמ״ש במ״א: **ראה בארוכה ד״ה שה תמים תרכ״ט. וש״נ.**

המדות שהם בבחי׳ צמיחה: **ראה תו״א בראשית צ, א ואילך. לקו״ת חקת נז, ב. נח, א. תו״ח בראשית יט, ד.**

בשעת השליחות יכול . . לקרוא א״ע בשם ה׳: **ראה תניא קו״א (קנט, א). אוה״ת וישלח רמח, ב. ויחי שנט, ב. ד״ה ויצב שם מזבח תרל״ג (סה״מ ח״א ע׳ מח ואילך). סה״מ תרנ״ה ע׳ נו. ובכ״מ.**

וזהו שארז״ל בדמ״ר פ׳ תרומה: **ראה גם ד״ה זאת חוקת תרכ״ט. וש״נ.**

כד קארי תרנגולתא: **ראה גם ד״ה הנותן לשכוי בינה בס׳ מאמרי אדה״ז תקס״ב ח״ב ע׳ שצד. ובתוס׳ הגהות באוה״ת מסעי ע׳ א׳שצד ואילך.**

וכמ״ש בזהר . . תרין שלהובין דנורא: **ראה אוה״ת מסעי שם. ובהמצויין ע״ז בהמשך מים רבים שם ובסה״מ תשי״א ע׳ 14.**

בד״ה מי יתנך ובהביאור וההגהות לשם: **לקו״ת שה״ש מד, ג. אוה״ת שה״ש ע׳ תרלו. תרנב. תרעו. וראה גם סה״מ תרכ״ו (הוצאת תשמ״ט) ע׳ קה.**

בלק״ת בשה״ש בד״ה יונתי בחגוי: **דף טז, ד. וראה גם האזינו עד, ד. ברכה צח, א. ובכ״מ.**

וכמאמר בעל העיקרים: **ראה עיקרים מ״א פכ״ג. מ״ד פ״ג. ובלקו״ת ראה כ, ד הובא בשם חכמי המחקר.**

ממ״ש במ״א מענין עפר שבקרקע המשכן: **ראה מאמרי אדה״ז תקס״ה ח״א ע׳ קמב. אוה״ת בראשית (כרך ג) תקכו, ב. בלק ע׳ תתקכ. תתקלב. תתקנד. ובכ״מ.**

הארי׳ למטה . . מבחי׳ הארי׳ שבמרכבה . . בדרך שבירה: **ראה בארוכה אוה״ת וארא ע׳ קסד. תו״א וישלח כה, ג. ביאוה״ז נ, ד. מאמרי אדה״ז תקס״ה ח״א ע׳ סא ואילך.**

ובאמת יש שורש הארי׳ . . למטה יותר: **ראה אוה״ת דרושים לחג השבועות ע׳ רכא. ד״ה זאת חוקת תרכ״ט.**

שארי׳ הוא אותיות ראי׳: **ראה תו״א ויחי מה, א. יתרו עא, ד. ובכ״מ.**

ולכן נק׳ החכמים עיני העדה: **ראה תענית כד, א בפרש״י ד״ה מעיני העדה. וראה אגה״ק סי״ד (קכ, ב). לקו״ת ואתחנן ב, סע״ד. ובכ״מ.**

ארי׳ שאג . . ואיתא בספרים שקאי על דבור אנכי: **ראה ד״ה זאת חוקת תרכ״ט (קרוב לתחילתו) ובהמ״מ שם.**

כשהי׳ משה בהר . . הי׳ יודע יום ולילה: **ראה גם יהל אור להצ״צ ס״ע סב ואילך.**

משל הקדמוני . . שהתורה היא משל . . קדמונו של עולם: **ראה ד״ה זאת חוקת תרכ״ט. וש״נ.**

ההפרש בין השתלשלות לבחי׳ בריאה יש מאין: **בענין ער״ע ויש מאין ראה גם לקו״ת דרושים לר״ה נו, סע״א ואילך. שה״ש מ, ב ואילך. ובכ״מ.**

ואם נאמר . . לא יש מציאת העולם . . נמצא שלא יש . . תומ״צ: **ויש לומר דזה שמביא בהמאמר שההוכחה שמציאות העולם היא מציאות אמיתית הוא מענין התומ״צ מרומז בזה גם שע״י עבודת האדם בלימוד התורה וקיום המצות נעשה קיום במציאות העולם שנעשית מציאות אמיתית (ד״ה זה היום תחלת מעשיך תשד״מ. עיי״ש).**

הושיט הקב״ה אצבעו הקטנה . . יותר מהחוק הקצוב: **ראה גם לקו״ת דרושים לר״ה ס, ב. ובכ״מ.**

מנהרות המכזבים . . אחת לשבע שנים . . פסולים: **פרה פ״ח מ״ט. והטעם לזה שכשנפסקין „לשנים רבות יותר משבע״** אינם **מים „מכזבין״ (רמב״ם הל׳ פרה פ״ו הי״ב. וראה תויו״ט במשנה שם) — י״ל: מכיון שכל מציאות העולם הוא „כזב״ (שהרי קיומו רק שית אלפי שנין ואח״כ חרוב), בהכרח לומר שכוונת הכתוב ב״מים חיים״ היא ל„חיים״ שבערך הבריאה גופא. ומכיון שכל שמיטה היא תקופה בפ״ע (ראה מפרשי התורה (ר״פ בהר) בטעם דאפקעתא דמלכא היא אחת לז׳ שנים), לכן ההפסק „לשנים רבות יותר משבע״ אינו נקרא „כזב״ בערך הקיום שבהבריאה (לקו״ש ח״ו ע׳ 92. וכ״ה בהדרן על הרמב״ם — משיחות י״ט כסלו תשל״ה, הערה 47).**

וז״ש הרמב״ם ע״פ וה׳ אלקים אמת: **הובא ונת׳ (נוסף להנסמן לעיל בתחלת המאמר) בהדרן על הרמב״ם שם. ובלקו״ש חכ״ז ע׳ 3-252.**

דברים הגשמי׳ הם אינם גשמי׳ . . עד״מ מציאת העץ . . הוא מורכב: **בהבא להלן עד סוף הפיסקא: ראה גם המשך תער״ב ח״ג ע׳ א׳תמב. ד״ה לדוד מזמור תרפ״ב פ״א (קונטרס מאמרים־תרפ״ב — ברוקלין, תשנ״ב, ס״ע 7-6).**

שכח ההסתר וכח המגביל הם אלקות כמו כח הבלתי בע״ג: **ראה גם סה״מ תרכ״ו (הוצאת תשמ״ט) ע׳ רז. סה״מ עת״ר ע׳ ל ואילך. תרפ״ט ע׳ 452 ואילך. תש״י ע׳ 62 ואילך.**

שרש הגבול הוא נעלה יותר . . כמ״ש במ״א מענין הרשימה: **אוה״ת וירא (כרך ז) תתשצג, ב. תצא ע׳ תתקכד־ה. וראה גם אוה״ת נח (כרך ו) תתרפח, ב. מים רבים תרל״ו פי״ג (ע׳ כ). וראה תו״א נח י, ד.**

וע׳ במ״א בענין רשימה חקיקה חציבה עשי׳: **מאמרי אדה״ז ענינים ע׳ שפח ואילך. וראה גם לקו״ת ויקרא נד, א. המשך תרס״ו ע׳ תקט ואילך. סה״מ עת״ר ע׳ לז. המשך תער״ב ח״א ע׳ רכח. סה״מ תש״י ע׳ 73.**

בסש״ב ח״ב פ״ג: **שעהיוה״א דף עח, א [ונקרא ג״כ בשם „ס׳ של בינונים ח״ב״ — אף שהשם סש״ב הוא בעיקרו על ח״א].**

אלמלא: **בשעהיוה״א שם: אילו.**

מאין ליש: **שם: מאפס ואין ליש.**

כגרזן ביד החוצב בו בלתי שום בחירה: **ראה תניא פל״ט (נב, רע״ב). אוה״ת נח שם תרנח, ב. סה״מ תר״ל ע׳ רסח. תר״ס ע׳ י. ד״ה כבוד מלכותך תשי״ב. ובכ״מ. וראה לקו״ש ח״ז ע׳ 14 הערה 22.**

לאב ואם שחלק הקב״ה כבוד . . להיותם בעלי בחירה: **ראה אוה״ת נח שם (כרך ג) תרנח, א ואילך. יתרו (כרך ח) ע׳ ג׳ג־ד. סה״מ תרנ״ח ע׳ קיח. ובארוכה לקו״ש חל״ו ע׳ 92 ואילך.**

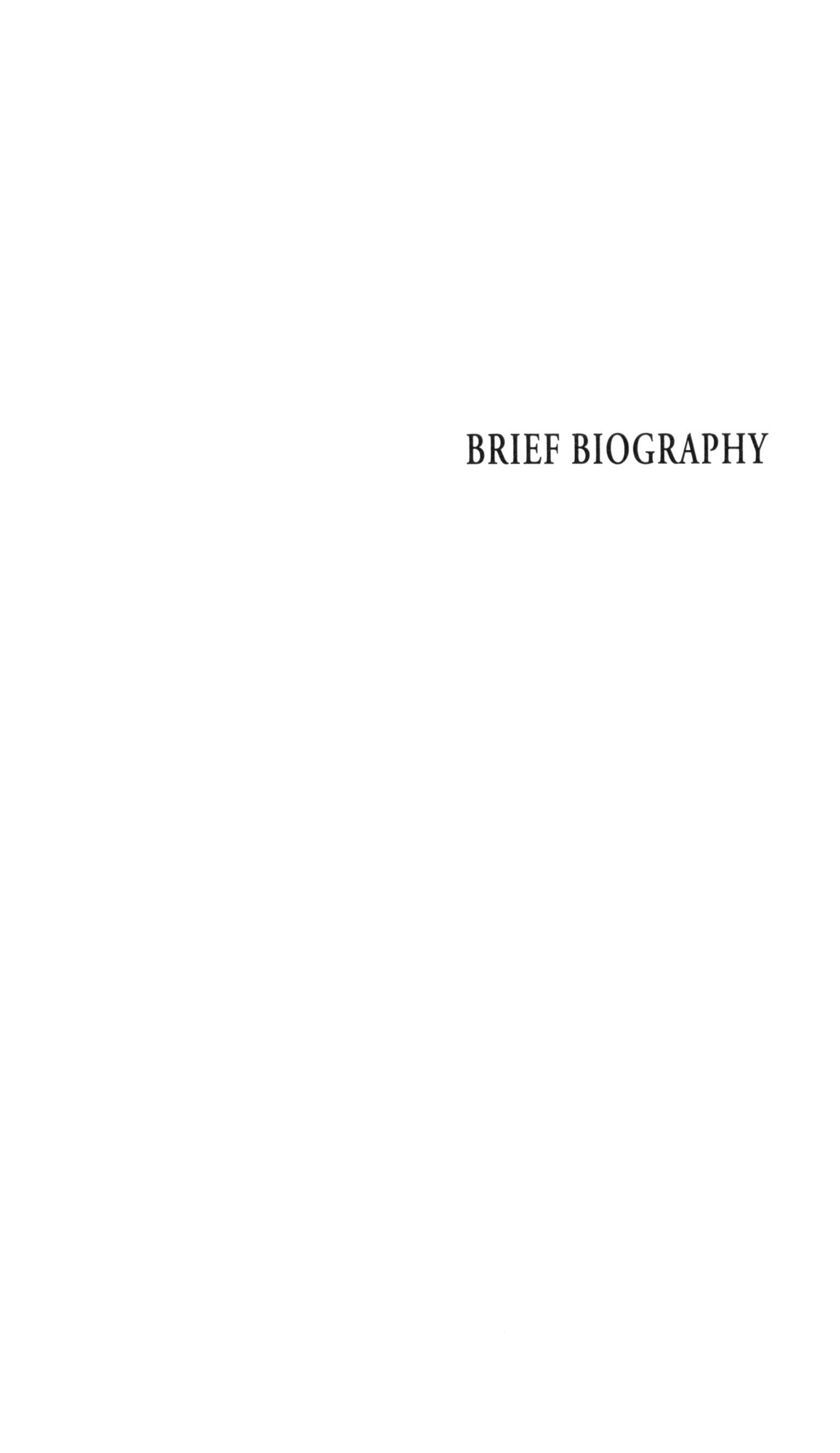

BRIEF BIOGRAPHY

Rabbi Shmuel Schneersohn
Fourth Rebbe of the Chabad-Lubavitch Dynasty (1834-1882)
Adapted from the writings of Rabbi Yosef Yitzchak of Lubavitch[1]

The Rebbe Maharash used to say:

The world says, "If you can't go under [an obstacle], go above it. And I say, from the start go above."

This saying epitomizes the attitude and modus operandi of the fourth Rebbe of Lubavitch. Rabbi Shmuel Schnersohn lived at a time when Russian Jewry was beset by persecution—from without and within. The Rebbe fought the causes of these persecutions with the attitude of one who remains aloof, above the fray. An obstacle to him was not something to be assessed and reckoned with. He gave it no credence and continued as if unaware on his path toward what he knew to be noble and true. L'chatchila ariber.

BIRTH

Lubavitch, Spring 1834. The Tzemach Tzedek's newly built home stood empty. It was the Rebbe's wish to wait until the holiday of Shavuot before moving in. His wife, Rebbetzin Chaya Mushka, had other plans. She was with child, her seventh and last son, and was quite resolute in her desire to give birth in her new home.

As her labor pains grew more acute, she made her way to the new house. A wooden bed used for sifting the Passover flour was covered with straw so that she could lie down.[2] Her husband was informed and hurried to her side. He instructed his three oldest sons to recite certain psalms in an adjacent room: psalms 1-4, 20-24, 33, 47, 72, 86, 90-3, 104, and 112-150. He instructed the midwife to

---

1. See *Otzar Sipurei Chabad*, vol. 8.

2. She would later tell her daughter-in-law: "What's the matter with you? I gave birth to "yours" on a 'sifting bed.'"

immerse in a *mikvah* before receiving the child. The child was to be received in a special white linen cloth that he had brought....

And so it was that on the second day of the month of Iyar, the day in which the attribute of Beauty[3] within Beauty (*Tiferet*-of-*Tiferet*) is dominant, exactly one hundred years after the light of the Baal Shem Tov began to illuminate the world, a son was born to Rebbetzin Chaya Mushka.

THE BRIS

Eight days later, the Tzemach Tzedek announced that the morning prayers would be recited in the early morning. By the hour of ten, all members of the family had already gathered, including the newborn's great-uncle, Rabbi Chaim Avraham, son of the Alter Rebbe.[4]

The hour of twelve came and went. The Tzemach Tzedek remained secluded in his holy chamber. The assembled grew anxious. A remark was heard from Rabbi Chaim Avraham: "No doubt he is entertaining guests of a greater stature than our own."

Half-hour later, the Tzemach Tzedek emerged, face glowing, eyes red with tears, a red handkerchief in his hand. "The *bris* will take place today," he announced. He lingered for a moment then returned to his holy chamber.

Rabbi Chaim Avraham approached the window, rested his head in his hands and was soon lost in thought. The sons of the Tzemach Tzedek exchanged Talmudic insights and chasidic thoughts while

---

3. The Rebbe was born on the second of Iyar, which is the 17th day of the 49 days of the *omer*, which are counted during the seven weeks between Passover and Shavuot. Each of the seven weeks embodies one of the seven basic emotions. Each day of a given week embodies that week's emotion as it is colored by one of one of the seven emotions. So the first day of the *omer* would be Kindness of Kindness, the second day would be Severity of Kindness, the third day Beauty of Kindness. The third day of the third week, then, is Beauty of Beauty. See Jacobson, *The Spiritual Guide to the Counting of the Omer* (Vaad Hanachos Hatmimim, 1996).

4. Rabbi Chaim Avraham rarely spoke. He was a tall and striking figure; his face was identical to his father's. A spirit of grace adorned his face. "When you looked at Rabbi Chaim Avraham," Rebbetzin Rivkah, wife of the Rebbe Maharash, related, "you felt good." He was phenomenally gifted and spent nearly all of his moments studying and praying. He displayed no interest at all in anything aside from Torah and Divine worship. He was of a generous nature and would greet every person with a smile.

the anxiety of the guests grew. The Rebbetzin dispatched a messenger to determine the cause of the delay but he was halted by Rabbi Chaim Avraham before he could enter the Rebbe's room.

After the hour of three, the Tzemach Tzedek once again emerged from his room. With joy shining from his face he announced again that the bris would take place that day, then returned to his room. At the hour of four he emerged again: "Do not yet recite the Mincha prayers; the bris will take place before long."

A short while later he again emerged and went to the room of the Rebbetzin. He discussed with her the name of the child then instructed that the child be readied for the circumcision.

During the circumcision the child cried profusely. The Tzemach Tzedek removed his hand from under the pillow that held the child and placed it on the child's head. The child immediately began to laugh and cried no more.[5]

THE NAME

The child was called Shmuel.

During the banquet, the Tzemach Tzedek's second son, Rabbi Yehudah Leib, turned to his father: "For whom is the child named? I don't recall any instance of such a name in our family." Then he added quietly, "Perhaps he is named after Shmuel the Prophet?"

The Tzemach Tzedek replied: "He is named after a water-carrier in Polotzk by the name of Shmuel. Indeed a wise person is greater than a prophet."[6] He also cited his grandfather, the Alter Rebbe, who said that the name Shmuel can be read as "*shemo E-l*—his name is G-d."[7]

---

5. At the bris of his grandson, Rabbi Yosef Yitzchak, the Rebbe Maharash quieted the child saying, "Why do you cry? When you will grow older, you will be a [Rebbe] and you will deliver Chasidus with ease." When Rabbi Yosef Yitzchak told this story he would leave out the word *Rebbe* out of deference to his father. His successor, the Rebbe, Rabbi Menachem Mendel, related that he had heard from chasidim what the missing word was.

6. *Bava Batra* 12a; *Zohar* I:7b.

7. In 1947, the Rebbe of blessed memory, wrote and published a biography of the Rebbe Maharash. In a letter to the sponsor of the publication, Rabbi Shmuel Karakowsky, the Rebbe noted this comment regarding the name Shmuel and added:

(See *Shelah* beginning of *Parshat Toldot* as well as gloss of *Chida* on *Zohar*

CHILDHOOD

He was a precocious and lively child. Being his father's youngest, as well as extraordinarily handsome, he enjoyed teasing his elders and they in turn loved to tease him.[8]

At the age of seven, he was already fluent in all of the *Chumash* as well as a good part of the Prophets and Writings. He was also studying Talmud with Rashi's commentary as well as selected comments of Tosafot. While playing with his friends, he would review verses of Torah from memory.

His father had the custom of testing him and his classmates (most of whom were family) once a month. Once, during one of these tests, the teacher was very impressed with the Rebbe's knowledge and said as much to the Tzemach Tzedek who replied: "What is the surprise when *Tiferet*-of-*Tiferet*[9] does well?"

After these monthly tests, the Tzemach Tzedek would give the children some coins. The Rebbe would use these coins—together with his weekly allowance—to buy books of Torah.

Once when Reb Noach Baruch the bookseller arrived in Lubavitch, the Rebbe went to his father to retrieve the coins that were

---

2:148b.) Perhaps this can be explained according to the explanation given by the Rebbe Maharash himself (in the series know as *V'kacha 1877*, ch. 10) regarding the statement of our Sages that the meaning of G-d's calling Jacob *Keil* is that He granted him a taste of the World to Come. For in the World to Come G-d will grant the righteous "310 worlds" and a tenth [i.e., a taste] of 310 is *Keil* [*alef-lamed*, which equals 31.] (It can be said that this is why the Rebbe Maharash was wealthy even in the physical sense, despite the fact that the righteous seek to dwell serenely in **this world**, but Satan argues that they will receive reward in the World to Come, see *Bereishit Rabbah*, beg. of 84. Indeed this is the literal meaning of "He grants them a taste of the World to Come," *Bava Batra*, end ch. 1.)

8. When he was five or six years old, a chasid teased him on *Shabbat Bereishit*, the first Shabbat to follow the festival-filled month of Tishrei. Said the child: "Chasidim know the significance of *Shabbat Bereishit*. But *mitnagdim* don't want to know. This Shabbat has a special grace." The chasid then asked him, "What is the difference between chasidim and *mitnagdim*?" To which he replied, "A *mitnagid* fears G-d; a chasid loves G-d."

Years later, his grandson, Rabbi Yosef Yitzchak, explained the remark of his grandfather: "When a person's relationship with G-d is based on fear alone, he is not personally invested (*nit mir nit dir*). But when a person loves G-d, he wants to know...."

9. See fn. 3.

held for him. But the Tzemach Tzedek told his son to first gain fluency in the books he already owned before buying new ones.

"When I entered Father's second room," the Rebbe later related, "and saw that the new bookcase delivered by Yosef Dovid the carpenter was full with books brought by Reb Noach Baruch and in addition there were four bundles of unbound books ready to be sent to Avraham Abba the bookbinder—I was heartbroken and said to Father, 'Are you already fluent in all the books you own? And yet you purchase new books every year. Just now when you returned from Petersburg you brought new books.'

"Father answered, 'As a general rule, I am fluent in the books I own. Choose any book you like and test me.'

"I did not think long and ran to one of the bookcases and took out the first book that came to my hand. When I removed the book, Father said, 'That is the *Mislol*, a book of grammar. Open the book and tell me the page number and I will tell you what is written there.' And so it was." The Tzemach Tzedek quoted the contents of the page verbatim.[10]

In the end, the Tzemach Tzedek gave him the money, adding another 10 ruble as a gift. The Rebbe purchased many books at that time.

"From a young age," said the Rebbe to his son, Rabbi Shalom Dovber, "I loved to read books of Torah. But I did not like the introductions written in florid language and rhymes, aside for the poetry of the early sages, whose every word is filled with the depths of wisdom."

* * *

In the summer of 5601, at the age of six, he began listening to the chasidic discourses of his father.

* * *

As a child, the Rebbe enjoyed the company of the elder chasidim and loved to hear their tales of years bygone. In a conversation with his son, the Rebbe recalls the first time he had seen the chasid

---

10. He did the same with the other books selected by his son: *Masoret Hamesorot*, also a grammar book; *Mesilot Hachochmah*, a book of Kabbalah; *Mesilat Yesharim*, a book of *mussar*; and *Masaot R' Binyamin*.

Rabbi Yitzchak Isaac of Vitebsk, one of the elder chasidim and in whom the Rebbe found a personal storyteller:

"When I was about eight years old, I saw Rabbi Yitzchak Isaac for the first time...I went to the shul and saw my great-great-uncle Reb Chaim Avraham and my great-uncle Reb Menachem Nochum together with three elder chasidim dancing in a circle. Tens of people, including my brothers and their children were standing around, singing and clapping.....

"I made my way through the crowd, ran [towards the dance circle], and held on to the *gartel* of one of the elders and danced with them. I noticed that my nephew, Reb Schneur Zalman, who was older than me by four or five years, envied my determination and confidence but I paid no attention to this.

"A month earlier, I had been ill with a throat illness, and was still frail. So after dancing for a while, I felt some pain and stopped. I stood over to the side and watched the dancing. I looked at Reb Chaim Avraham and saw that tears were streaming down his cheeks, his eyes shut tight, his brow wrinkled, his lips mumbling as one recalling various memories.

"When the dancing ended, Rabbi Yitzchak Isaac hugged and kissed Reb Chaim Avraham and Reb Menachem Nochum...."

The Rebbe continued telling his son:

"I always had good luck. As a child, I was very good at finding favor in others. Even the elder chasidim indulged me with stories and ideas.

"So as soon as I heard from Rabbi Yitzchak Isaac that he had seen the Alter Rebbe at the beginning of his leadership, and that he had studied in the *chadarim* established by the Alter Rebbe, and that he knew many stories, I befriended him. Whenever he would come to Lubavitch, I would spend many hours with him. Over the course of 23 years, 5603-5626, I heard many stories and other matters from him."[11]

---

11. "Rabbi Yitzchak Isaac had a phenomenal memory. When he recalled an event that occurred during his childhood, eighty or eighty five years in the past, he would recall the name of the place as well as the names of the individual characters that were present then. The way he spoke, you could tell that the events he was retelling stood vividly before his eyes."

STUDY

At the age of 10, the Rebbe was placed under the tutelage of a brilliant Torah scholar, Rabbi Shalom of Kidan. In addition, he would study for about four hours twice a week with his older brother, Reb Yisrael Noach, also a brilliant Torah scholar.

During that year, some of the greatest Rabbinic authorities of the day came to Lubavitch to discuss communal affairs. One of the rabbis, Rabbi David Luria, debated with the Rebbe on a topic the Rebbe was studying—and the 10-year old outdid the venerable sage.

At the age of 12, in addition to his studies with Rabbi Shalom, he spent much time committing a great deal of *Mishanyot* to memory.

Once his father noticed him copying discourses and said that this was not an appropriate job for him. The Rebbe replied that he had already finished all of his studies and that his mind was tired.

His father responded: "When I was nine years old, I had a set study schedule and Grandfather would check my progress. After one particular test, he gave me some material to study but I was tired from my previous studies. I also wanted to be outside in the fresh air, so I put off my studies for later and went outside. When Grandfather saw through the window that I was outside, he called me and asked me why I was not studying the material he had given me. I said that I had already exhausted my mind with my previous study. Grandfather then took his walking stick, placed it on my shoulder, and said: "Here is Understanding for you, here is Openness of Heart (*petichat halev*) for you."

* * *

From the Rebbe's recollections of that period:

"That winter, Father gave me a hand-written copy of the discourse entitled "*The root of the mitzvah of prayer*" to study before my Bar-mitzvah. I transcribed a copy for myself and in the process learned to imitate Father's handwriting...

"Over the course of a few months, I learned to write quite well, and I would transcribe all that I heard from Father. I would also transcribe all the stories I heard from chasidim, since Father had told me that at my age he would try to sit in the company of elder chasidim to hear their conversations....

"In the middle of the winter, Father began studying *Tanya* with me....I diligently committed *mishnayot* to memory. I was fluent in the first five books of the *Mishna* and a few tractates of the book of *Taharot*. For Father had told me that for my Bar Mitzvah I should be perfectly fluent in all six books of the *Mishna*, all of *TaNaCh*, as well as *Tanya*."

* * *

The Rebbe received much affection and extra attention from his father. Once, when he was twelve or thirteen, he went into his father's office at a late hour of the night. His father had just finished with his private audiences, which had taken longer than usual that night. In the course of their conversation, his father complained, "What do they want from me? I could have been studying during all this time!"

The Rebbe did not respond. He went over to the bookcase, removed the curtain, and began counting the volumes of his father's writings. He counted more than 30 volumes. He turned to his father: "Would you have been able to write so many discourses if you would not receive people for private audience?"

"Indeed, you are right," his father replied.

MARRIAGE

At the age of 14, he married his niece, Rebbetzin Sterna. Tragically, the bride fell ill during the seven-day celebration after the wedding. She lay ill for three months then passed away.

To assuage the pain of the greatly distressed young widower, the Tzemach Tzedek instructed that the Rebbe be given the room adjacent to his office so that he would have access to him at any time. The Tzemach Tzedek would show his son manuscripts of chasidic writings, even those that he would not show to his other sons.

The following Elul and Tishrei, the Rebbe kept to himself and immersed himself in his studies.

The following winter, he took part in the rabbinic assembly, which was convened in Vitebsk.

The next year, he was engaged to his cousin Rebbetzin Rivkah, an orphan. (As a child, he had once said that she would be his bride. The family laughed at the time and called them "groom and bride.")

At the engagement celebration, Rebbetzin Rivkah's older sister said to the Tzemach Tzedek: "No doubt we have gotten ourselves a fine match. Even if our father was still alive and he offered a dowry of ten thousand rubles he could never have gotten such a match. But know that you have done better than us. I boast not of our distinguished pedigree as descendants of the *Eishel Avraham*[12] and our other holy ancestors; you have a fine pedigree of your own. But whereas we have acquired you as our in-law, you have acquired the Father of Orphans as your in-law. May He bless the couple with *mazal tov.*"

The Rebbetzin's childhood had been one of suffering and sadness and her marriage to the Rebbe brought her into a new world, one of happiness and bliss.

* * *

A year or so later, at the age of 17, the Rebbe was instructed by his father to receive rabbinic ordination. He was subsequently ordained by some of the greatest sages of the time.

At the age of 18, he began a steady schedule of study with his father. In the winter, they would study from ten to midnight and during the summer they would study from four to six thirty in the morning. This went on for 14 years save two months. During the first two years, they studied kabbalistic works with chasidic interpretation. For 18 months they studied the classic works of Jewish philosophy: Rabbi Saadiah Gaon, *Guide for the Perplexed*, *Kuzari* and others—all with the interpretation of *chasidism.*

* * *

"When I was 19 years old," the Rebbe once told his son, "I fell ill. I was visited many times by the specialist, Dr. Heibenthal, and when I was no longer in critical condition I had to remain in bed for some three months. During that time, Father would visit me each day and sit with me for about two hours, sometimes three of four.

"Generally, he would recount his memories of his grandfather's

---

12. Rabbi Avraham ben Shaul Broida (c. 1650-1717), world-famous Rabbi of Metz and Frankfurt, and head of a *Yeshivah* in Prague. He is known by the title of his work, *Eishel Avraham*, which features novel insights to the Talmudic tractates of *Pesachim*, *Chulin*, and *Bava Batra*. *Eishel Avraham* was published in Frankfurt, 1747.

house and he told me stories about his grandfather in the court of his master, the Maggid of Mezrich."

* * *

At the age of 20, he was instructed by his father to become involved in communal affairs. That year his father sent him in his stead to a government meeting of Jewish leaders in Petersburg. Throughout the next few years and indeed throughout his life, his communal responsibilities took him on a number of trips within Russia as well as abroad (Italy, Germany, France).[13] To avoid suspicion, a rumor was circulated that the Rebbe's trips were made to improve his ill health.[14]

(After returning from one of his trips to Germany, at the age of 24, he was asked by his father for his impressions of the German Jews. The Rebbe replied: "They are *yifei mareh* ('handsome')."

His grandson, Rabbi Yosef Yitzchak, explained this as a backhanded criticism: "When a German Jew gets up in the morning he will not have his coffee before reciting his prayers. On the wall in the shul hangs a schedule with the exact time for the prayers. During the week the prayers are to take 18 minutes, and on Monday and Thursday—days when the Torah is read in the synagogue—22 minutes. A German Jew donates a tenth of his earnings to charity—but only when he has made a profit. That's a *yifei mareh.*

"A Russian Jew may not be a *yifei mareh,* but he is full of life. When he begins to pray, he doesn't know how long it will take—half an hour, an hour and a quarter. And he gives charity regardless of whether he's made a profit....")

PROGENY

The Rebbe and his wife had six children: four boys and two girls.

Their eldest, Devorah Leah, was born in the early 1850s and was

---

13. He was fluent in many languages: Russian, French, Latin, and others.

14. The Rebbe suffered poor health throughout his life. He was advised by his doctors to work with his hands. He subsequently built many pieces of furniture that displayed extraordinary craftsmanship. He built a 13-branched candelabra that was the size of a man. He also built tables made of small pieces of wood and mosaic stone and the like. One of these tables is still extant, and stands in the room of the Rebbe, Rabbi Menachem Mendel, of blessed memory.

an extremely wise child. She kept the same study schedule as that of her brothers.[15] Once, during the meal of *Acharon shel Pesach* (the final day of Passover), her brother, Rabbi Shalom Dovber, asked their father why the last day of Passover is celebrated as a *yom tov.* The Rebbe said to his eldest son, "Zalman Aaron, maybe you can answer his question?" He replied that he did not know. Devorah Leah was sitting near her mother and said she did know: "...All Jews celebrate the fact that they made it through the festival of Pesach without committing the grave sin of *chametz* on Pesach." Her father was very pleased with this answer and said, "Devorah Leah, you have a 'good head.' "[16]

Their second child, Reb Avraham Sender, passed away at the tender age of eight years. He was exceptionally gifted. The Tzemach Tzedek said of him that he possessed the soul of the Alter Rebbe. At the age of four, the Tzemach Tzedek taught him *Mishna* and the young prodigy would anticipate all the comments of the *Gemara.* He was an extremely sincere child. It was not in him to waste time. He was always busy studying and praying. At his deathbed, he amazed all present with his calm demeanor. On the day of his passing he said that the Alter Rebbe had appeared to him and said that he would be joining him in heaven. He therefore wished to be dressed in Shabbat clothing. He prayed Mincha with great joy. After *Aleinu,* he said *Shema Yisrael* and as he said the words *Hashem echad,* his soul departed.

Their third child, Reb Schneur Zalman Aaron, was born on 19 Tammuz, 5618. The Tzemach Tzedek called him by his acronym RaZA, applying to him the phrase in the Zohar, "this is the hidden *raza* (secret)."

Their fourth child, Rabbi Shalom Dovber, was born 20 Cheshvan 5621. He later succeeded his father as Rebbe.

Their fifth child, Rabbi Menachem Mendel, was born six years later on 6 Adar.

Their youngest child, Chaya Mushka, was born in the late 1860s.

* * *

---

15. *Sefer Hasichot 5696* p. 139.

16. *Sefer Hasichot kayitz 5700*, p. 71.

At the age of 31, the Rebbe was instructed by his father to begin delivering chasidic discourses publicly. The Tzemach Tzedek sent a note to his chasidim that read, "To him shall you listen, as you have listened to me."

An undated letter from his father that apparently dates from that time reads as follows:

To my dear and cherished son, may you live and be well,

I have seen your chasidic writings and they find much favor in my eyes. G-d should strengthen your heart and mind to add strength in His Torah and service. Be strong and be a man. Open your mouth and may your words illuminate. I wish to assure you of what I told you orally, and as I told you what I heard from my grandfather. Be strong and courageous to write and speak. And I empower you with great empowerment. Do not fear any man. And may G-d grant you success in both the material and the spirit—to learn, to teach, to keep and to fulfill.

Your father who seeks your welfare and the welfare of our brotherhood,
Menachem Mendel son of Devorah Leah

The Tzemach Tzedek had also said to his son: "The spiritual flask of oil that the Baal Shem Tov gave to the Maggid of Mezrich with which to anoint the Alter Rebbe as leader to his generation—it was with this strength that my father-in-law was anointed, and with this strength I anoint you."

The following summer, the Tzemach Tzedek passed away.[17]

TRANSITIONS

After his father's passing, the Rebbe remained in Lubavitch and assumed leadership of the Lubavitch community.

---

17. Even after his father's passing, the Rebbe continued to communicate with him. His wife, Rebbetzin Rivkah, related:

"Generally, he would go outside the city twice a day. At some point he would get off the carriage and sit among the trees. There the souls of his forebears would reveal themselves to him and he would converse with them. Many times he predicted the future based on what they had told him. Before going to the grave of his father, he would ask me if there was anything I wished to request or know. When he would return, he would say, "this is what father answered…."

Like the other chasidic masters, the Rebbe held private sessions—called *yechidut*—with his chasidim. "The main difficulty with yechidut," he once confided, "is the constant 'dressing and undressing.'" He was referring to the need to enter the psyche of one chasid, then leave that perspective and enter that of the next chasid. Rabbi Yosef Yitzchak calls this procedure "a toil of the soul."

When the chasid would present the traditional note containing the chasid's request for specific blessings, the Rebbe would read it and respond immediately, providing the chasid with a blessing and advice. He would then add some aphorism, tailored to the character of the particular chasid, to inspire and guide him in his divine worship and character development. "These aphorisms," said Rabbi Yosef Yitzchak, "remained as guiding lights for the chasidim throughout their lives."

COMPASSION

His love and care for his fellow was remarkable. He once exclaimed: "What is the value of *chasidut* and piety if the main thing, love of one's fellow, is lacking even to the extent of causing pain, G-d forbid, to another!"

His father once told him:

"When you help another person make a living, even to help him earn just 70 *kopeks* on a calf, all the gates of the supernal chambers are open before you."

A few years later, the Rebbe Maharash repeated this to his son and added:

"One ought to know the route to the supernal chambers, though it is not crucial. All you need is the main thing—to help your fellow with a complete heart and with sensitivity, to take pleasure in doing another person a favor."

Before prayer, he would often seek out a pauper and give him food. Citing the custom of the Talmudic sage Rabbi Elazar, who would "give a coin to a pauper and then pray,"[18] he explained:

"Prayer must be alive. By giving alms to a pauper before praying—thereby giving him life—your prayer gains much vitality." As

18. *Bava Batra* 10a.

he said this, he raised his hand upward to indicate that the increase of vitality is unimaginable.

ILLNESS

The Rebbe suffered from various illnesses throughout his life.

In the winter of 5635 (1875), the Rebbe felt so ill that he composed a will.

> *"...though I am still in my middle years...nevertheless, I am already weakened from the illnesses that I have suffered. I now suffer from a weak heart.... I hope that G-d in His great mercy will lengthen my days and years, for I am now in my 41st year....*
>
> *"First and foremost I instruct my sons and daughters to be extremely careful in honoring your mother, my wife, may she live and be well...*
>
> *"Strengthen yourselves to study the Torah, both its revealed and hidden dimension. Two thirds of the day shall you spend in the study of the revealed Torah, and one third in the hidden Torah. On Shabbos, two thirds hidden and one third revealed....*
>
> *"'The sum of the matter, when all is considered: G-d shall you fear and his mitzvot shall you keep. For this is the whole of man.'[19] ...Be G-d-fearing without flaunting it to others...Your inside and the inside of your inside should be paved with awe and love of G-d...."*

"CAPITALIST JEWS"

The Rebbe spent much of his time traveling abroad and within Russia in an effort to ameliorate the spiritual and physical conditions of life for the Jews in Russia.

In 1879, various elements within Russia began to incite the masses towards a pogrom. The Rebbe then traveled to Petersburg and was assured by a number of government officials that the incitement would cease. Later, when a pogrom did break out in Kiev and Niezhin, the Rebbe secured a meeting with the Minister of Interior. The Rebbe reminded the minister of his promise to put an end to the incitement and mentioned that such behavior towards Jews was likely to raise quite an outcry abroad.

---

19. Ecclesiastes 12:13.

The minister replied that he was well aware of the political power of the "capitalist Jews" abroad but he was also aware of the lack of any close feelings between them and the Jews of Russia, and their lack of sympathy—even hostility—for the rabbis.

The Rebbe firmly protested the minister's remarks, saying that the minister was obviously ignorant of the psychological nature of the Jew and oblivious to their brotherly love.

The Rebbe said: "I have received numerous letters from those "capitalist Jews" abroad, who have great political power, and want to know how to relate to the saddening news coming out of Russia about the Jews there. They want to know what they can do to ensure the safety of Jewish lives and property in Russia."

"And what did you answer?" the minister asked angrily.

"I will refrain from answering them until I receive a response from the government regarding my efforts in the matter."

"Lubavitcher Rebbe! You are threatening the Russian government with the capitalist Jews abroad."

"The minister need not take my words as a threat. But he should consider the matter quite serious and that even many non-Jewish capitalists will support it, since humanity in general must react strongly against such barbaric deeds."

"Will the Lubavitcher Rebbe with the help of the capitalist Jews abroad instigate a revolution in Russia?"

"That will be brought on in time by the officials of the Russian government themselves with their bureaucratic and irresponsible leadership."

That day the Rebbe was placed under house arrest in the Hotel Serapinsky for two days. When he was released, he made his way to the minister to ask for an answer. He was told that he would have an answer in two weeks.

The Rebbe's efforts bore fruit and for some time the Jews of Russia enjoyed complete calm.

KTO ZDYES RABIN?

His modus operandi in public service gained him more than a few sworn enemies among the other Jewish leaders of the time. He never sought their advice nor paid them any notice. He maintained that the Jewish leadership ought to speak frankly and boldly with government officials and suffer the consequences. He spoke his mind and was not inhibited by the wealth of the barons or the pseudo-sophistication of the "enlightened ones."

Indeed, the Rebbe was often the target of unwanted attention. In 1878, on the way to one of his trips abroad, he passed through Dvinsk, where many of his opponents made their dwelling. They arranged for an enormous crowd to come to the station so that the Rebbe would suffer some discomfort. By the time the Rebbe arrived, the crowd, which could not be contained by the confined space of the station, had damaged many of its windows and doors.

Dvinsk was then under siege and the general in charge was informed of the incident. He gave an order to arrest the Rebbe. When the official who came to carry out the arrest announced, "*Kto zdyes rabin* (Who is the Rebbe here)?" those standing around the Rebbe retreated in fear. The Rebbe then removed a document from his pocket and showed it to the official. Upon seeing the document the official began to quake with fear and stood before the Rebbe like a servant before his master. When the Rebbe said to him that he wished to write down his name and number, the official turned white. In the end, the general himself came to ask the Rebbe's forgiveness.

The document was from Petersburg and stated that all police officials should provide the Rebbe any assistance that he might need.

CLEAN HANDS

When he traveled abroad in 1880, he asked his nephew, Rabbi Yeshaya Berlin, to accompany him along with a few young men. However, because of the incident in Dvinsk, Rabbi Yeshaya, who lived then in Velisz, did not take this request seriously. Being occupied with other matters, he sent R. Yaakov Rashal, of Riga, in his stead. When R. Yaakov arrived, the Rebbe said to him, "It is good that you have come. Buy a train ticket, first class, and accompany me for a few stops." When they entered the train, the Rebbe told him to remain with him in his cabin. In the meantime, a young man entered the cabin carrying a traveler's bag and sat down opposite the Rebbe. The Rebbe turned to him and said: "A Jew need not have the

hands of Esau. Give me what you have." The young man removed a pistol from his pocket and handed it to the Rebbe. The Rebbe took the pistol and tossed it out the window. He then turned to R. Yaakov and said, "Now you can go back."

PARISIAN RETREAT

His care for his people was not limited to grand communal issues. In one Baal-Shem-Tov-like episode, he traveled to Paris for the sake of one man's soul:

The Rebbe once made a trip to Paris, accompanied by Rabbi Yeshaya and others. When they arrived in Paris, Rabbi Yeshaya asked the Rebbe, "Uncle, where to?"

"To the Alexander." (The Alexander was one the largest hotels in Paris and was the hotel of choice for kings and nobles.) When they arrived at the hotel, the Rebbe, speaking a fluent French, asked for a suite of rooms on the same floor as the casino.

A few hours later, the Rebbe made his way to the casino and sat down near a young man playing cards. From time to time the young man would take a sip of wine from his glass. The Rebbe placed his hand on the young man's shoulder and said, "Young man, one is not allowed to drink non-kosher wine." Then he said, "Non-kosher wine dulls the mind and heart—be a Jew!" He concluded with, "Have a good night" and left the room emotionally stirred.

(Rabbi Yeshaya later commented that he had never seen the Rebbe in such an excited state.) In his excitement, the Rebbe unwittingly sat down on one of the chairs used to carry hotel guests from one floor to the other. (These would later be replaced by the elevator.) Members of the hotel staff immediately came over to the Rebbe and lifted the chair. When the Rebbe realized what was happening he begged their "*pardon*" and went to his room.

A few hours later, the young man appeared at the Rebbe's room and inquired after the man that had spoken to him. He was led into the Rebbe's room and remained there for some time. On the morrow, the Rebbe left. He later commented that it was many generations since a soul of such purity had come to this world, though it had been buried in the depths of depravity. The fellow later adopted a lifestyle more consistent with the loftiness of his soul...

ROYALTY

And so the Rebbe filled the days of his relatively short life: studying and teaching Torah and Chasidut, guiding and educating his chasidim, and improving the plight of the physically and spiritually downtrodden, both far and near.

He did this all in the manner of *lichatchila ariber*, a motto that permeated all of his actions. His physical life too was lived in such a way. In contrast to other Rebbes, who generally shunned material wealth, he is known to have lived quite lavishly. His home, which he designed himself (after the great fire in Lubavitch in 1868), was distinguished by its spacious rooms, large windows, and unusually high ceilings (which contrasted sharply with the architecture of the day). He traveled in an elegant carriage drawn by four horses and wore expensive clothing. When his father would receive an expensive gift, he would often pass it on to his regal son.

Obviously, these luxuries were not meant for his own self-aggrandizement or indulgence. Rather, as an utterly transparent servant of G-d, he was able to employ the riches of the world for their true purpose: to bring praise to the Name of G-d. As the Talmud says of gold: the sole purpose of its creation was that it be used to beautify the Holy Temple.[20]

At a Purim farbrengen in 1968, the Rebbe of blessed memory, told the following regarding the Rebbe Maharash:

Every morning he would rise very early and daven. Then he would go for a ride in his carriage, driven by a special coachman, into the forest.

The coachman, a non-Jew, was instructed never to reveal the nature of these forays into the forest. Chasidim being chasidim, however, pestered the man enough (or got him so drunk) until he blurted out: "*Chednay chilavek* ("strange man"). He comes to the forest, sits down under a tree and begins to cry. Then, [biting] ants cover him from all sides and he continues to cry. He does not chase them away. Then, suddenly, all the ants run away and he stops crying. He gets back into the carriage and we go back home. *Chednay chilavek.*

---

20. Another chasidic Rebbe known for such lavishness was the Rebbe of Ruzhin, a close friend of the Tzemach Tzedek. See also fn. 7.

Shto uhn platchet? (Why is he crying?). What is he lacking? A carriage, he has. A driver, he has. A wife and children, he has. Silver watches and a golden cane, he has. Yet he leaves his palace, sits down in the middle of the forest under a tree, allows the ants in the entire vicinity to crawl all over him and cries. *Kazhdee dyen* (everyday). And then, inexplicably, the ants all run off him, suddenly, not because of something he does but of their own accord…."

(When the Rebbe Maharash found out that the driver had revealed the secret, he instructed his attendants to fire him. But after crying and promising never to reveal any secrets, he was allowed to remain on.)

FINAL DAYS

At the Rebbe's *bris*, his father had said cryptically, citing Psalms: "'*The days of our lives—in them* [bahem] *are seventy [years]*….'[21] There are a few types of years: Eighty [years], seventy, and the numeric equivalent[22] of *bahem* when including the letters themselves [which equals 50]."

Some fifty years later, in the spring of 1882, the Rebbe sighed and said: "Father said *bahem* with its letters—that means 50 years…."[23]

Toward the end of the year 5642 (1882), he fell critically ill. On the 13th of Tishrei 5643, at 12:26, the Rebbe, sitting on his chair, took out his pocket watch and changed the time to 12:51. He rolled up a small piece of paper and inserted it into the watch, halting its movement. He then summoned his children and spoke with them one at a time. At 12:51 he passed away. He was 48 years old.

In accordance with his instruction, he was buried in Lubavitch, right near his father the Tzemach Tzedek.

Yet more than a century later his legacy of *l'chatchila ariber* lives on—in the minds, hearts and deeds of chasidim throughout the world. May his memory be for us a blessing. Amen.

---

21. Psalms 90:10.

22. See fn. 80 & 100 of the *maamar*.

23. The Rebbe Maharash passed away at the age of 48. However, his life spanned 50 calendar years when one includes the year he was born and the year he passed away.

IMPORTANT DATES

IMPORTANT DATES IN THE LIFE OF RABBI SHMUEL

5594 (1834): Birth of Rabbi Shmuel on 2nd of Iyar. His first marriage—5608 (1848)—was with the daughter of his brother, Rabbi Chaim Schneur Zalman, and his second was with Rebbetzin Rivka in 5609 (1849).

5615 (1855): Begins communal activities.

5617 (1857): Travels to Petersburg on communal matters.

5619 (1859): Travels to Germany to confer with communal leaders.

5623 (1863): Travels to Kiev, rescues hundreds of families on the verge of being expelled from Volhynian villages.

5625 (1865): Travels to Petersburg, succeeds in nullifying a decree submitted to the Senate limiting rights of Jews in Lithuania and Zamut.

5626 (1866): Accepts post of Rebbe.

5628 (1868): Travels to France to confer with communal leaders.

5629 (1869): Organizes a permanent committee in Petersburg to follow matters of communal interest.

5640 (1880): Endeavors successfully to halt the pogroms.

5643 (1882): Passes away on the eve of Tuesday, 13 Tishrei, and is interred in Lubavitch.

His sons:

1) Rabbi Schneur Zalman Aaron.
2) Rabbi Shalom DovBer.
3) Rabbi Avraham Sender.
4) Rabbi Menachem Mendel.

His daughters:

1) Rebbetzin Devorah Leah; married Rabbi Moshe Aryeh Leib Ginzburg.
2) Rebbetzin Chaya Mushka; married Rabbi Moshe Horenstein.

PUBLISHED WORKS

PUBLISHED WORKS OF RABBI SHMUEL

1. *Likkutei Torah Al Gimmel Parshiot.*
2. *Torat Shmuel – Sefer 5626.*
3. *Torat Shmuel – Sefer 5627.*
4. *Torat Shmuel – Sefer 5628.*
5. *Torat Shmuel – Sefer 5629.*
6. *Torat Shmuel – Sefer 5630.*
7. *Torat Shmuel – Sefer 5631, 2 vol.*
8. *Torat Shmuel – Sefer 5632, 2 vol.*
9. *Torat Shmuel – Sefer 5633, 2 vol.*
10. *Torat Shmuel – Sefer 5634.*
11. *Torat Shmuel – Sefer 5635, 2 vol.*
12. *Torat Shmuel – Mayim Rabbim, 5636.*
13. *Torat Shmuel – Sefer 5636 vol. 2.*
14. *Torat Shmuel – Sefer 5637, 2 vol.*
15. *Torat Shmuel – Sefer 5638.*
16. *Torat Shmuel – Sefer 5639, 2 vol.*
17. *Torat Shmuel – Sefer 5640, 2 vol.*
18. *Torat Shmuel – Sefer 5641.*
19. *Torat Shmuel – Sefer 5642.*
20. *Torat Shmuel – Derushei Chatunah.*
21. *Igrot Kodesh.*

English Translations:

22\. *True Existence, 5629.*

23\. *Channeling the Divine, 5634.*

22\. *Feminine Faith, 5640.*

INDEX

INDEX

A

H

N

O

T

TITLES IN THE CHASIDIC HERITAGE SERIES

THE ETERNAL BOND

FROM TORAH OR

Translated by Rabbi Ari Sollish

This discourse explores the spiritual significance of *brit milah*, analyzing two dimensions in which our connection with G-d may be realized. For in truth, there are two forms of spiritual circumcision. Initially, man must "circumcise his heart," freeing himself to the best of his ability from his negative, physical drives; ultimately, though, it is G-d who truly liberates man from his material attachment.

JOURNEY OF THE SOUL

FROM TORAH OR

Translated by Rabbi Ari Sollish

Drawing upon the parallel between Queen Esther's impassioned plea to King Ahasuerus for salvation and the soul's entreaty to G-d for help in its spiritual struggle, this discourse examines the root of the soul's exile, and the dynamics by which it lifts itself from the grip of materialism and ultimately finds a voice with which to express its G-dly yearnings. Includes a brief biography of the author.

TRANSFORMING THE INNER SELF

FROM LIKKUTEI TORAH

Translated by Rabbi Chaim Zev Citron

This discourse presents a modern-day perspective on the Biblical command to offer animal sacrifices. Rabbi Schneur Zalman teaches that each of us possesses certain character traits that can be seen as "animalistic," or materialistic, in nature, which can lead a person toward a life of material indulgence. Our charge, then, is to "sacrifice" and transform the animal within, to refine our animal traits and utilize them in our pursuit of spiritual perfection.

KNOWLEDGE AND FAITH

FROM LIKKUTEI TORAH

Translated by Rabbi Eli Kaminetzky

As true as the fact that the mind and its elements are gifts from G-d, so does faith inspire us in a way that mere accumulation of knowledge cannot. Faith's inspiration lifts us beyond the boundaries of our finite existence, yet, that inspiration can depart just as easily as it came. Knowledge, however, becomes a part of us and thus changes us decisively. In effect, faith and knowledge complement and balance each other. This discourse discusses the fundamental concept of faith in G-d as compared to the imperative to "know" G-d, and the differences between the two.

RABBI DOVBER OF LUBAVITCH

FLAMES

FROM SHAAREI ORAH

Translated by Dr. Naftoli Loewenthal

This discourse focuses on the multiple images of the lamp, the oil, the wick and the different hues of the flame in order to express profound guidance in the Divine service of every individual. Although *Flames* is a Chanukah discourse, at the same time, it presents concepts that are of perennial significance. Includes the first English biography of the author ever published.

RABBI MENACHEM MENDEL OF LUBAVITCH,
THE TZEMACH TZEDEK

THE MITZVAH TO LOVE YOUR FELLOW AS YOURSELF

FROM DERECH MITZVOTECHA

Translated by Rabbis Nissan Mangel and Zalman I. Posner

The discourse discusses the Kabbalistic principle of the "collective soul of the world of *Tikkun*" and explores the essential unity of all souls. The discourse develops the idea that when we connect on a soul level, we can love our fellow as we love ourselves; for in truth, we are all one soul. Includes a brief biography of the author.

THE ART OF GIVING

FROM OR HATORAH

Translated by Rabbi Shmuel Simpson
Edited by Rabbi Avraham D. Vaisfiche

What's the ideal way to give tzedakah? Specifically, is it best to give whatever we can at any given time regardless of the amount, or should we postpone our tzedakah giving until such time as we can afford to make a more sizable contribution? Or is neither approach necessarily preferable to the other? This discourse emphatically exclaims that, yes, it does indeed make a difference how we go about giving to tzedakah, because the experience of tzedakah is about so much more than meets the eye.

RABBI SHMUEL OF LUBAVITCH

TRUE EXISTENCE

MI CHAMOCHA 5629

Translated by Rabbis Yosef Marcus and Avraham D. Vaisfiche

This discourse revolutionizes the age-old notion of Monotheism, i.e., that there is no other god besides Him. Culling from Talmudic and Midrashic sources, the discourse makes the case that not only is there no other god besides Him, there is nothing besides Him—literally. The only thing that truly exists is G-d. Includes a brief biography of the author.

TRUE EXISTENCE

THE CHASIDIC VIEW OF REALITY

A Video-CD with Rabbi Manis Friedman

Venture beyond science and Kabbalah and discover the world of Chasidism. This Video-CD takes the viewer step-by-step through the basic Chasidic and Kabbalistic view of creation and existence. In clear, lucid language, Rabbi Manis Friedman deciphers these esoteric concepts and demonstrates their modern-day applications.

CHANNELING THE DIVINE

ITTA B'MIDRASH TILLIM

Edited by Rabbi Avraham D. Vaisfiche

The Bar Mitzvah, the day a Jewish boy turns thirteen, is a turning point in his life. He comes of age, becoming responsible for adher-ence to the *mitzvot*—and everyone celebrates. Chabad Chasidim mark this milestone by having the "Bar Mitzvah boy" publicly deliver a discourse, originally delivered by Rabbi Shalom DovBer Schneersohn, fifth Lubavitcher Rebbe, on the occasion of his Bar Mitzvah in 5634 (1873). Its main theme is the cosmic impact of performing the mitzvah of *tefillin*, and the special connection between this mitzvah and the age of Bar Mitzvah.

FEMININE FAITH

L'HAVIN INYAN ROSH CHODESH, 5640

Translated by Rabbi Shais Taub

When the Jews served the Golden Calf during their sojourn in the wilderness, says the Midrash, the women refused to join them. This discourse traces the roots of the feminine within the supernalrealms, and explores its relationship to women and how it translat-ed into their aversion for unholy and ungodly worship. Why are women more sensitive than men to G-d's role in earthly events and His mastery over Creation? The answer explores G-d's unity and immanence in the world, and the innate sensitivity that women posses to spirituality.

RABBI SHALOM DOVBER OF LUBAVITCH

DIVINE SPEECH

YOM TOV SHEL ROSH HASHANAH 5659 DISCOURSE ONE

Translated by Rabbis Yosef Marcus and Moshe Miller

The discourse explores the attribute of *malchut* and the power of speech while introducing some of the basic concepts of Chasidism and Kabbalah in a relatively easy to follow format. Despite its title and date of inception, the discourse is germane throughout the year. Includes a brief biography of the author.

FORCES IN CREATION

YOM TOV SHEL ROSH HASHANAH 5659 DISCOURSE TWO

Translated by Rabbis Moshe Miller and Shmuel Marcus

A fascinating journey beyond the terrestrial, into the myriad spiritual realms that shape our existence. Rabbi Shalom DovBer systematically traces the origins of earth, Torah and souls, drawing the reader higher and higher into the mystical, cosmic dimensions that lie beyond the here and now, and granting a deeper awareness of who we are at our core.

THE POWER OF RETURN

YOM TOV SHEL ROSH HASHANAH 5659 DISCOURSE THREE

Translated by Rabbi Y. Eliezer Danzinger

This discourse examines the inner workings of *teshuvah*, and explains how it is precisely through making a detailed and honest examination of one's character and spiritual standing—which inevitably leads one to a contrite and broken heart—that allows one to realize his or her essential connection with G-d.

OVERCOMING FOLLY

KUNTRES UMAAYAN MIBEIT HASHEM

Translated by Rabbi Zalman I. Posner

In this classis ethico-philosophical work, Rabbi Shalom DovBer weaves Chasidic doctrine, Kabbalah thoughts, Biblical and Talmudic texts and candid insights into human frailties into a document structured and systematic, yet informal and personal—a text for study and meditation.

TRACT ON PRAYER

KUNTRES HATEFILLAH

Translated by Rabbi Y. Eliezer Danzinger

Tract on Prayer expounds on the concept of *tefillah*—prayer, as understood in Chabad Chasidic philosophy. Building on the Talmudic dictum that prayer constitutes the "service of the heart," *Tract on Prayer* captures the quintessence of *tefillah* as the vehicle for attaining attachment to G-d. It guides the worshiper in preparing for this divine service of the heart, setting out the role and dynamics of contemplation before and during prayer. *Tract on Prayer* also explores various Kabbalistic and Chasidic concepts.

THE SIMPLE SERVANT

UMIKNEH RAV 5666

Translated by Rabbi Yosef Marcus

This discourse elaborates upon three types of personalities with distinct approaches to Divine service: 1) The child of G-d, naturally committed; 2) The loyal servant of G-d, motivated by his appreciation of G-d; 3) The simple servant of G-d, driven by his acceptance of the yoke of Heaven. His apathy makes serving G-d difficult. Yet he does his work consistently because he is reaching beyond himself—overcoming his own nature.

ALL FOR THE SAKE OF HEAVEN

PADA BESHALOM 5668

Translated by Rabbi Zalman Abraham

Delivered on the Chasidic holiday of Yud Tet Kislev, the Nineteenth of Kislev, in the year 5668 (1907) and opening with the verse *Pada Beshalom Nafshi*, the discourse discusses the correct approach to mundane human activities, such as eating, drinking, and business dealings, so that these can be carried out truly for the sake of Heaven.

EXPLORING THE SOUL

V'CHOL ADAM 5679

Translated by Rabbi Shmuel Simpson

An analysis of the biblical verse which forbids any man from being present in the sanctuary when the High Priest entered to seek atonement. If, as the verse in Leviticus states: "No man shall be in the Tent of Meeting" at that time, how could the High Priest himself be present? By *exploring the soul*, its composition, and transcendent levels, the discourse explains how the High Priest, on Yom Kippur, ascended to the sublime level of "no man," thus granting him the permission and sanction to enter the Holy of Holies.

RABBI YOSEF YITZCHAK OF LUBAVITCH

THE PRINCIPLES OF EDUCATION AND GUIDANCE

KLALEI HACHINUCH VEHAHADRACHAH

Translated by Rabbi Y. Eliezer Danzinger

The Principles of Education and Guidance is a compelling treatise that examines the art of educating. In this thought-provoking analysis, Rabbi Yosef Yitzchak teaches how to assess the potential of any pupil, how to objectively evaluate one's own strengths, and how to successfully use reward and punishment—methods that will help one become a more effective educator.

THE FOUR WORLDS

FROM IGROT KODESH

Translated by Rabbis Yosef Marcus and Avraham D. Vaisfiche
Overview by Rabbi J. Immanuel Schochet

At the core of our identity is the desire to be one with our source, and to know the spiritual realities that give our physical life the transcendental importance of the Torah's imperatives. In this letter to a yearning Chasid, the Rebbe explains the mystical worlds of *Atzilut*, *Beriah*, *Yetzirah*, and *Asiyah*.

ONENESS IN CREATION

KOL HAMAARICH B'ECHAD 5690

Translated by Rabbi Y. Eliezer Danzinger

Said by Rabbi Yosef Yitzchak at the close of his 1930 visit to Chicago, this discourse explores the concept of Divine Unity as expressed in the first verse of the *Shema*. The discourse maintains that it is a G-dly force that perpetually sustains all of creation. As such, G-d is one with creation. And it is our study of Torah and performance of the mitzvot that reveals this essential oneness.

CREATION AND REDEMPTION

HACHODESH 5700

Translated by Rabbi Yosef Marcus

Tishrei celebrates Creation, the birth of the world, indicative of the natural order. Nissan commemorates the miraculous Exodus from Egypt, or the supernatural. In human terms, when struggling with the obfuscation of the natural, the key is to recognize the dimension where the limitations of the natural order do not exist. In fact, the physical exists only so that we may demonstrate how it too exposes the Divine truth. And when we recognize this, we can realize the supernatural even within the natural.

THE MAJESTIC BRIDE

LECHA DODI 5689 / 5714

Translated by Rabbis Ari Sollish and Avraham D. Vaisfiche

Customarily recited by a groom at the Kabbalat Panim reception, *Lecha Dodi* traces the Kabbalistic meaning of the order of the wedding ceremony, when first the guests welcome the groom, and then walk with the groom to welcome the bride, at which point the groom covers the bride's face with the veil. The discourse cites a number of examples and other situations where similar procedures occur, finally applying the reasoning to groom and bride to understand the Kabbalat Panim ceremony and the purpose of marriage.

RABBI MENACHEM M. SCHNEERSON,
THE LUBAVITCHER REBBE

ON THE ESSENCE OF CHASIDUS

KUNTRES INYANA SHEL TORAS HACHASIDUS

This landmark discourse explores the contribution of Chasidus to a far deeper and expanded understanding of Torah. The Rebbe analyzes the relationship Chasidus has with Kabbalah, the various dimensions of the soul, the concept of Moshiach and the Divine attributes.

FULL DEVOTION

LO TIHYEH MESHAKELAH 5712

Translated by Rabbi Zalman Abraham

Referred to as a landmark discourse, delivered by the Rebbe barely two years after ascending to the leadership of Chabad-Lubavitch, this discourse is perhaps unique among all of the Rebbe`s teachings in the sense that its message required a retooling of our conception of divine service. It discusses the self-satisfaction that might result from our love and awe of G-d, and that contemplating the fact that our days upon earth need to be utilized to the fullest serves to remove any such feelings of satisfaction.

RECURRING EXODUS

BECHOL DOR VADOR—VEHECHERIM 5734

Translated by Rabbi Yehuda Altein

These two Chasidic discourses explore the deeper dimensions of the Exodus, and teach how one can experience the transition from slavery to freedom on a daily basis. More than just a geographical region, "Egypt" represents any obstacle that limits our ability to be our real selves and reach our true potential. When we succeed and break free of our own limitations, we are liberated from own Egypt, and experience our own Exodus. For this sentiment to endure, we, too, must "pass through the sea on dry land," which refers to bringing awareness of G-d even to areas where it had previously been concealed.

GARMENTS OF THE SOUL
A DAY OF STRENGTH

VAYISHLACH YEHOSHUA 5736
28 SIVAN 5749

Translated by Rabbis Yosef Marcus and Levi Friedman

Often what is perceived in this world as secondary is in reality most sublime. What appears to be mundane and inconsequential is often most sacred and crucial. Thus, at their source, the garments of the human, both physical and spiritual, transcend the individual.

THE UNBREAKABLE SOUL

MAYIM RABBIM 5738

Translated by Rabbi Ari Sollish

No matter how much one may be inundated with materialism, the flame of the soul burns forever. A discourse that begins with an unequivocal declaration, it speaks to one who finds pleasure in the material world, yet struggles to find spirituality in his or her life.

VICTORY OF LIGHT

TANU RABANAN MITZVAT NER CHANUKAH 5738

Translated by Rabbi Yosef Marcus

Even darkness has a purpose: to be transformed into light. This discourse explains how we can draw strength from the story of Chanukah for our battle with spiritual darkness, so that we, like the Macabees of old, may attain a *Victory of Light*.

THE PATH TO SELFLESSNESS

YEHUDAH ATAH 5738

Translated by Rabbi Shmuel Simpson

Beginning with the words *Yehuda Atah*, the discourse examines the blessing which Yaakov blessed his fourth son, Yehuda, as compared to the blessings he gave his first three sons, Reuven, Shimon and Levi. Yaakov's sons embody distinctive forms of divine service, which correspond to distinct sections of the prayers of Shema and the Amidah. Using these distinctions, the discourse further derives lessons about the bond between the individual Jewish soul and G-d.

NURTURING FAITH

KUNTRES PURIM KATTAN 5752

Translated by Rabbi Yosef Marcus

At its core, this discourse discusses the function of a *nassi*, a Jewish leader, who awakens within every single person the deepest part of the soul. Similar to Moses, the *nassi* inspires the person so that one's most basic faith in G-d leaves the realm of the abstract and becomes real. *Nurturing Faith* will cultivate your bond with the Rebbe's role as the Moses of our generation.

STAYING THE COURSE

A COLLECTION OF DISCOURSES BY THE CHABAD REBBES ON THE INSEPARABLE BOND BETWEEN REBBE AND CHASID

Translated by Rabbi Shmuel Simpson

Discussing various ways through which the Chasid can continue to nurture and renew this bond, the discourses presented in this work speak to the seasoned Chasid as well as those newly introduced to the Rebbe and his teachings.

There are many important manuscripts that are ready to go to press, but are waiting for a sponsor like you.

Please consider one of these opportunities and make an everlasting contribution to Jewish scholarship and Chasidic life.

For more information please contact:

The Chasidic Heritage Series
770 Eastern Parkway
Brooklyn, New York 11213
Tel: 718.774.4000
editor@kehot.com

In memory of

Hanoch Pinchus ben Aharon ז״ל

Alter ben Akiva ז״ל

Akiva ben Yonah ז״ל

Betzalel ben Yisroel ז״ל

Leilah bas Avraham ז״ל

And in honor of

Dorit bas Leilah שתחי׳

Luba bas Brocha שתחי׳

And in honor of

Yud Kislev, 5781

לחיזוק ההתקשרות **לכ"ק אדוננו מורנו ורבינו**

ולזכות **שניאור זלמן** בן **בת שבע בינה** וכל משפחתו
שיחיו לאורך ימים ושנים טובות, לברכה והצלחה בכל הענינים,
לבריאות טובה, שלום בית, נחת חסידותי, ופרנסה בהרחבה בגו"ר

In loving memory of

Dr. Hinda L. Krinsky

מרת **הינדא לאה** ע"ה בת ר' **מנחם מענדל** שי'

לעילוי נשמת

רחל בת דבורה ע"ה

In Honor of Dov Ber שי' Nathanson

On the occasion of his Upshernish

Yossi & Yael Nathanson

לעילוי נשמת ריזל רבקה בת הרב משה יחיאל ע"ה

לזכות נעה אסתר, אליהו יהושע, חיה שמחה, ויונה משה דוד שיחיו ברמן

In honor of Willy David Ascher – from his grandchild Mats Önner

In honor Hinda Rochel bas Zlata Gitel for good health and long life till 120

In honor of the Rabbis and Rebbetizens of Mequon, WI

All those in need of Refuas Hanefesh and Refuas Haguf

לע"נ הוריי יוסף בן יקותיאל הכהן וליבא מירל בת יעקב ע"ה

In memory of Rav Menachem Mendel Hakohen ע"ה Feldman

In Honor of Moshe Ben Rachel for Menuchat Hanefesh

In honor of the marriage of Elizabeth Lavin to Aaron Levine

לזכות שלום דובער בן חוה ודבורה לאה בת בתשבע וכל יו"ח שיחיו

בזכות אמונה ובטחון וגאולה

Anonymous

In honor of the Rebbe and his light that continually shines

In memory of Shelley Kaplan

לזכות פייגא דבורה חיה מושקא בת שושנה שתחי'

May Hashem bless the Shut family with spiritual, mental, and physical health

In honor of Menachem Mendel ben Avraham Nissin

הוצאת ספרים
קרני הוד תורה
קה"ת
ליובאוויטש